animal man

ORIGIN OF THE SPECIES

animal man

ORIGIN OF THE SPECIES

Grant Morrison Writer

Chas Truog Tom Grummett Pencillers

Doug Hazlewood Steve Montano Mark McKenna Inkers

Tatjana Wood Helen Vesik Colorists

John Costanza Janice Chiang Letterers

Brian Bolland Original series covers

Karen Berger	VP-Executive Editor
Karen Berger Mark Waid	Editors-original series
Art Young	Assistant Editor-original series
Scott Nybakken	Editor-collected edition
Nick J. Napolitano	Associate Editor-collected edition
Robbin Brosterman	Senior Art Director
Paul Levitz	President & Publisher
Georg Brewer	VP-Design & Retail Product Development
Richard Bruning	Senior VP-Creative Director
Patrick Caldon	Senior VP-Finance & Operations
Chris Caramalis	VP-Finance
Terri Cunningham	VP-Managing Editor
Stephanie Fierman	Senior VP-Sales & Marketing
Alison Gill	VP-Manufacturing
Rich Johnson	VP-Book Trade Sales
Hank Kanalz	VP-General Manager, WildStorm
Lillian Laserson	Senior VP & General Counsel
Jim Lee	Editorial Director-WildStorm
Paula Lowitt	Senior VP-Business & Legal Affairs
David McKillips	VP-Advertising & Custom Publishing
John Nee	VP-Business Development
Gregory Noveck	Senior VP-Creative Affairs
Cheryl Rubin	Senior VP-Brand Management
Bob Wayne	VP-Sales

ANIMAL MAN: ORIGIN OF THE SPECIES

DC Comics, 1700 Broadway, New York, NY 10019
A Warner Bros. Entertainment Company
Printed in Canada. Second Printing.
ISBN: 1-56389-890-X
Cover illustration by Brian Bolland
Color reconstruction on pages 6-24 by Lee Loughridge
Publication design by Louis Prandi

Animal Man™

by Morrison, Truog & McKenna

THE REVEILLE, WHEN IT SOUNDED, WAS BOTH UNFORESEEN AND LOUD.

IT BEGAN AS A DEEP SEISMIC PULSE IN THE COREHEART OF THE TRAVELLER.
A PULSE WHICH SURELY MUST HAVE CAUSED SOME DISTURBANCE IN THE WORLD ABOVE.

I MUST CONFESS, I HAD FULLY EXPECTED TO SLEEP UNTIL THE ARRIVAL OF THE AEONIC UNIT BUT THAT, IT SEEMED, WAS NOT TO BE.
I GATHERED THE NAKED NUMBERS OF MY BEING AND RECORPORATED INTO THE FIRST AVAILABLE MEMORYFORM.

ALL THE WHILE, THE PULSE CONTINUED, ARRHYTHMIC, UNMUSICAL.
SOMETHING WAS CLEARLY WRONG.

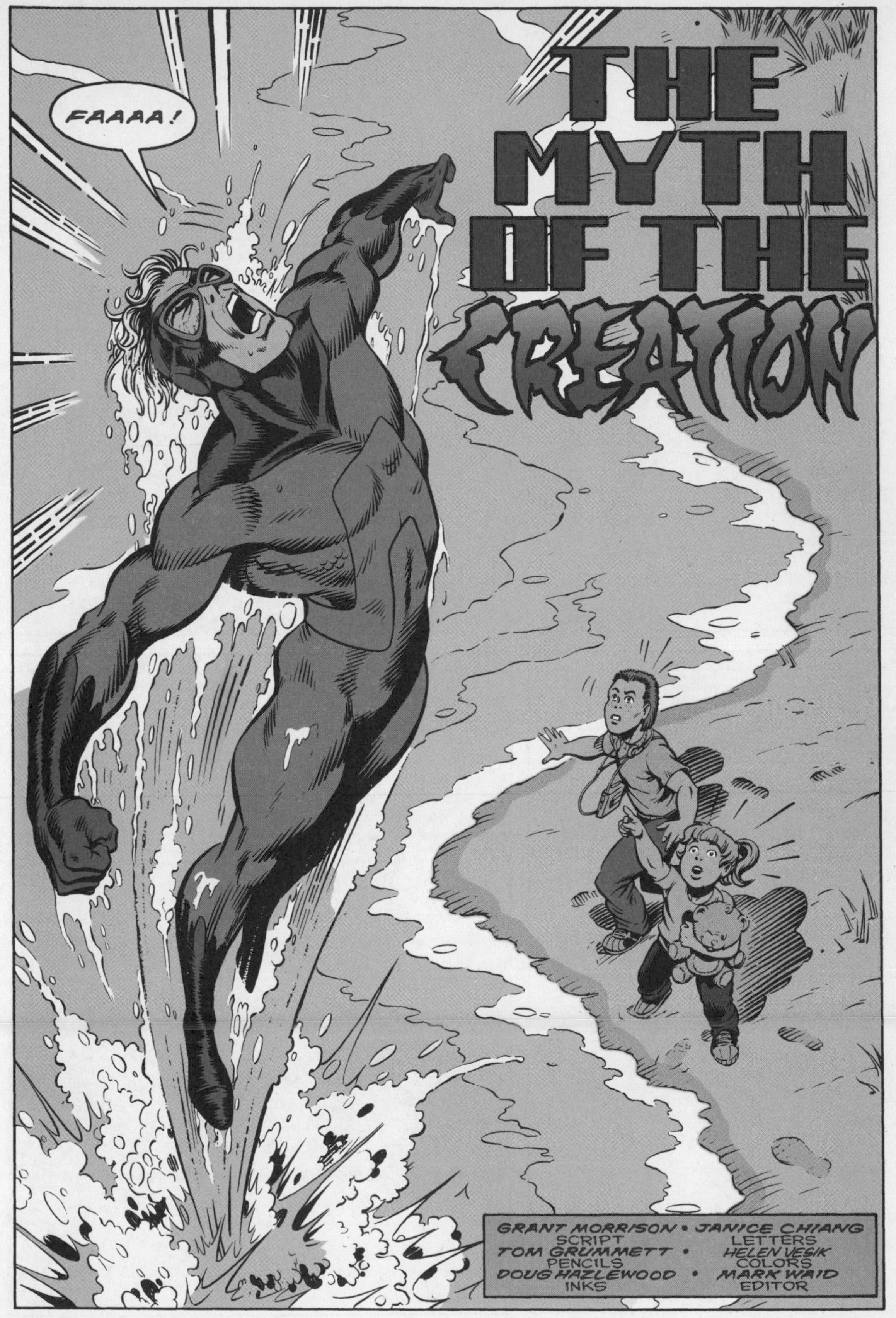
FAAAA!
THE MYTH OF THE CREATION
GRANT MORRISON • JANICE CHIANG
SCRIPT LETTERS
TOM GRUMMETT • HELEN VESIK
PENCILS COLORS
DOUG HAZLEWOOD • MARK WAID
INKS EDITOR

WELL?...

AH, IT'S NO USE.
I SEEM TO BE ABLE TO FLY OKAY JUST BY CASTING OUT BLINDLY... BUT EVERYTHING ELSE IS TOTALLY SCRAMBLED.

I COULDN'T BREATHE UNDERWATER AT ALL.
I TRIED TO ABSORB SOME FISH POWERS, BUT ALL I GOT WERE SIGNALS FROM A WOODCHUCK SOMEWHERE EAST OF HERE.

IT'S THE SAME WITH EVERYTHING. I TRY TO TAKE ANT POWERS AND INSTEAD I GET...OH, I DON'T KNOW... A HORSE HALF A MILE AWAY OR SOMETHING.
WHAT'S WRONG WITH ME?

THIS IS ALL I NEED, ELLEN! I FINALLY MADE IT INTO THE JUSTICE LEAGUE AND THIS HAS TO HAPPEN.

I MEAN, LOOK! WATCH THIS!

I'LL TRY TO PICK UP SOME DOG ABILITIES FROM SKIPPER, OKAY?
NOW JUST WATCH!

BUDDY, IS SOMETHING...

WRONG...

SEE? WHAT DID I TELL YOU?...

FLEAS!

HEY, DAD! LOOK WHAT WE FOUND!
YEAH, I'LL SEE IT IN A MINUTE, CLIFF.
DAD'S NOT FEELING TOO GOOD RIGHT NOW.

NO, I'M OKAY. I JUST FEEL KINDA WASHED-OUT THESE DAYS...
MAYBE YOU'VE GOT M.E.. YOU KNOW, POST VIRAL SYNDROME...

THE YUPPIE DISEASE?
COME ON, ELLEN! DO I LOOK LIKE A YUPPIE?

TWO THINGS: FIRSTLY, THE TRAVELLER HAS BEEN DISCOVERED BY HUMANS. SECONDLY, OUR 'ANIMAL MAN' AS YOU SEE, HAS SOMEHOW BEEN ALTERED ALMOST BEYOND RECOGNITION.

THE FIRST PROBLEM IS CURRENTLY BEING DEALT WITH. AS FOR THE SECOND... PERHAPS YOU'LL UNDERSTAND NOW WHY THE TRAVELLER FELT IT NECESSARY TO DESLEEP US.
YES.

HE'S YOUNGER, ISN'T HE?
HE'S BECOME YOUNGER.

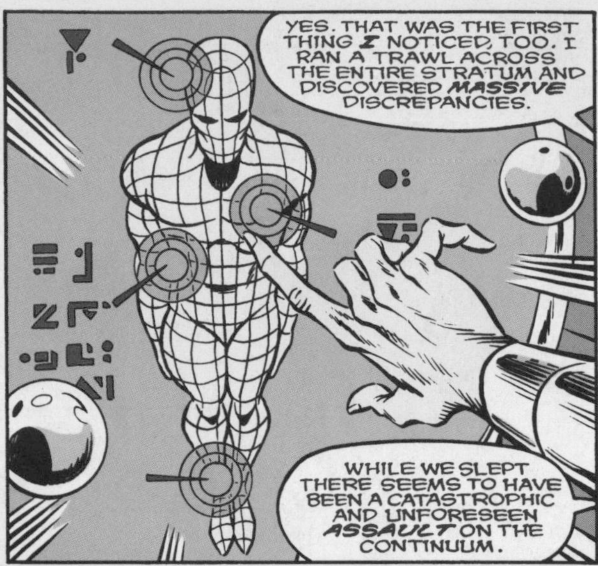
YES. THAT WAS THE FIRST THING I NOTICED, TOO. I RAN A TRAWL ACROSS THE ENTIRE STRATUM AND DISCOVERED MASSIVE DISCREPANCIES.
WHILE WE SLEPT THERE SEEMS TO HAVE BEEN A CATASTROPHIC AND UNFORESEEN ASSAULT ON THE CONTINUUM.

YOU'LL NOTICE ALSO THAT 'ANIMAL MAN' HAS BEEN RENDERED ALL BUT INOPERATIVE. SOME RECENT EVENT HAS UNDONE OUR MORPHOGENETIC GRAFTS AND CUT HIM LOOSE FROM THE AVATAR BESTIARY.
WITHOUT ATTENTION, HE MAY DIE SOON.

THE GRAFTS CAN BE REPAIRED. I'M MORE CONCERNED ABOUT WHAT HAS HAPPENED TO THE CONTINUUM WHILE WE WERE ASLEEP.
I THINK WE SHOULD REVIEW THE CREATION OF 'ANIMAL MAN' AS WE REMEMBER IT.

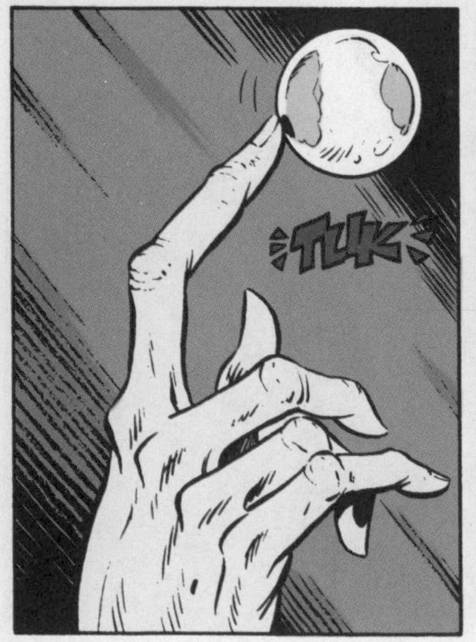
TLIK

PERHAPS THIS WILL HELP US TO ASSESS THE EXTENT OF THE DAMAGE.

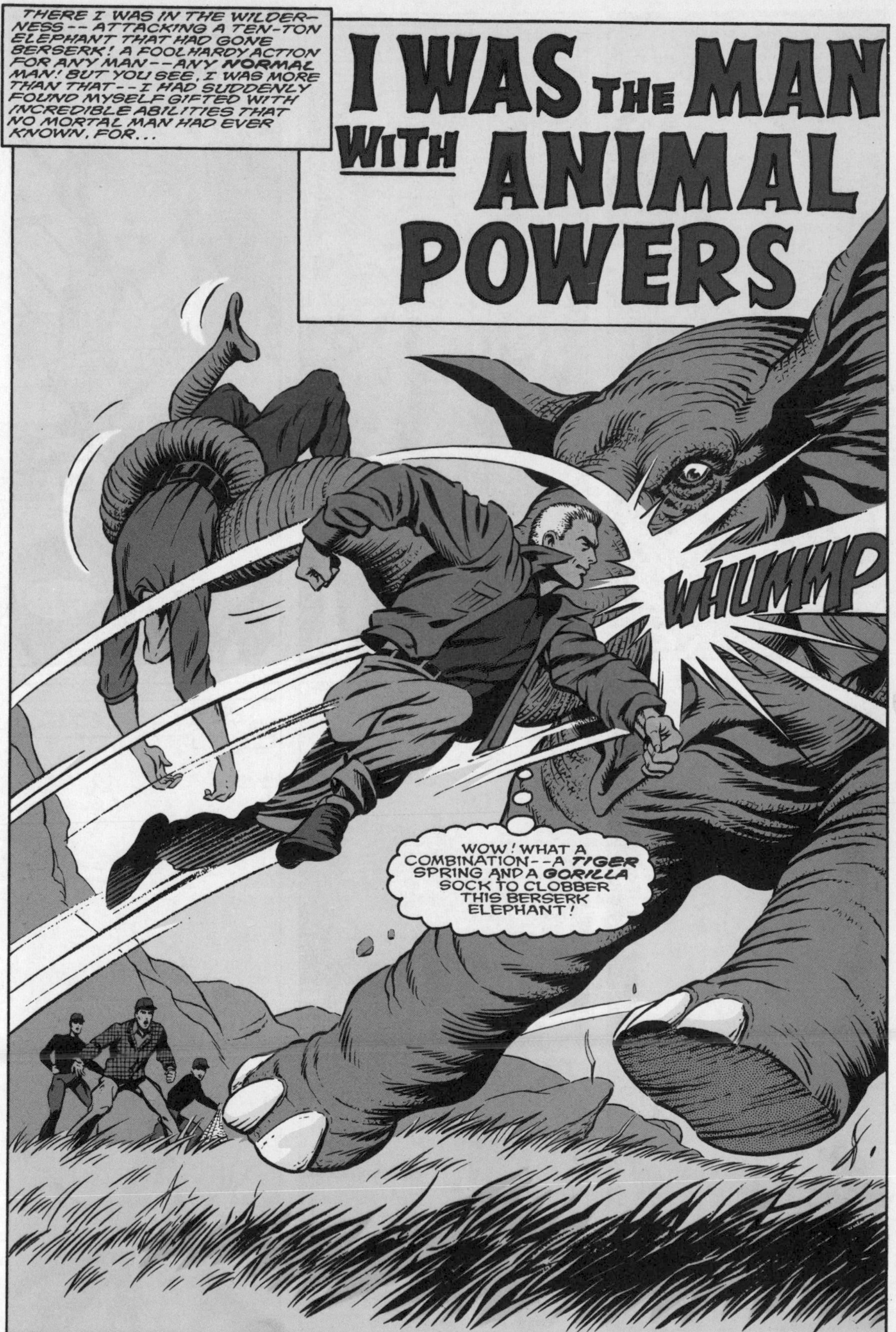
THERE I WAS IN THE WILDERNESS -- ATTACKING A TEN-TON ELEPHANT THAT HAD GONE BERSERK! A FOOLHARDY ACTION FOR ANY MAN -- ANY NORMAL MAN! BUT YOU SEE, I WAS MORE THAN THAT -- I HAD SUDDENLY FOUND MYSELF GIFTED WITH INCREDIBLE ABILITIES THAT NO MORTAL MAN HAD EVER KNOWN, FOR...
I WAS THE MAN WITH ANIMAL POWERS
WHUMMP
WOW! WHAT A COMBINATION--A TIGER SPRING AND A GORILLA SOCK TO CLOBBER THIS BERSERK ELEPHANT!

I LIKED TO THINK OF MYSELF AS A GUY WITH A TIGER IN HIS TANK, BUT WHEN IT CAME TO PROPOSING, WELL...

I GUESS YOU COULD SAY I WAS A MOUSE OF A MAN...
ELLEN... I WANT TO... WELL, ER, THERE'S SOMETHING I... WHAT I MEAN TO SAY IS...

OH, BUDDY, Y-YES?...
...I...

AH, IT'S NOTHING. FORGET IT. IT'S NOT IMPORTANT.
GUESS I'D BETTER BE GETTING ALONG NOW...

DID IT AGAIN--I LOST MY NERVE!
SOME TIGER!

I COULD HEAR MYSELF SQUEAKING ALL THE WAY HOME.

AND I TOOK THE INEVITABLE NEEDLING NEXT DAY WHEN I WENT OUT HUNTING.
HAH! CHICKENED OUT AGAIN, HUH? YOU'RE ONE HECK OF A ROMEO, BUDDY-BOY!
YEAH, OKAY, OKAY--YOU'VE HAD YOUR LAUGH, ROGER! NOW, WHY DON'T WE SPLIT UP AND HUNT TRACKS?

I'LL TAKE THE RIDGE TRAIL...
AS LONG AS YOU THINK YOU CAN HANDLE THE WILDLIFE, HERO!
THERE ARE SOME REAL MEAN BUNNIES UP THERE!

ROGER COULD LAUGH ALL HE LIKED.

WE'D SOON SEE WHO'D BE EATING RABBIT PIE TONIGHT.

KA-BOOM

M-MY EYES... CAN'T SEE...CAN'T...

I DON'T KNOW HOW LONG I WAS OUT OR WHAT HAPPENED TO ME BUT WHEN I WOKE UP, I WAS FLAT ON MY BACK...
...OH...

THEN SUDDENLY I HEARD A SOUND...
GROOWWW

AND I FOUND MYSELF GAPING AT A FOUR-FOOTED NIGHTMARE...
A-A TIGER! IN THIS COUNTRY?...

ARROOO
...SPRINGING AT ME...I'M A GONER...

IN A BLIND PANIC, I INSTINCTIVELY LEAPT TO ONE SIDE-- AND THEN IT HAPPENED.
HUH?... I'M SPRINGING OFF THE GROUND... LIKE...LIKE A...

...LIKE A TIGER!...
THIS IS CRAZY... NOTHING'S MAKING ANY SENSE... I...

AAARG
YI! NOW A GORILLA WANTS TO PLAY TAG WITH ME!

I WAS CAUGHT BETWEEN THE DEVIL AND THE DEEP BLUE SEA.

THEN THE TIGER SPRANG AND I REACHED OUT TO PROTECT MYSELF.
AS MY HANDS SNARED THE BEAST'S PAWS, I FELT A TREMENDOUS STRENGTH SURGE THROUGH MY ENTIRE BODY, AND...
UNNH!
WHERE DID I GET SUCH POWER? I TOSSED THAT TIGER WITH THE STRENGTH OF A... A GORILLA!
BUDDY! HEY, BUDDY!
NET THOSE ANIMALS WHILE THEY'RE STILL DAZED!
I SURE AM GLAD TO SEE YOU STILL BREATHING, PAL!
THERE WAS A TRAIN WRECK BACK THERE-- SOME CIRCUS ANIMALS ESCAPED...
...I THOUGHT I WAS GOING CRAZY FOR A WHILE...
BUT WHAT ABOUT THESE ANIMAL POWERS? THERE WAS AN EXPLOSION...
I WAS UP THERE ON THE RIDGE AND THERE WAS A LIGHT...
YEAH, I SAW A GLOW EARLIER. WE'D BETTER TAKE A LOOK!
HEY! THERE IS SOMETHING DOWN THERE, BUDDY!

WHY...IT'S AN ALIEN SPACE CAPSULE! THAT'S WHAT CAUSED THE EXPLOSION!
OF COURSE-- AND THE RADIATION GLOW MUST HAVE AFFECTED ME IN SOME WAY, GIVING ME THE CHARACTERISTICS OF ANY ANIMALS IN MY GENERAL VICINITY!

THERE'S SOMETHING TOUCHING ABOUT THE BLIND FAITH WITH WHICH THEY GREET THE IMPOSSIBLE.
IT'S ALWAYS BEEN THE SAME ON THIS STRATUM: RADIATION, CHEMICAL ACCIDENTS, MAGIC RINGS. THE PHYSICAL LAWS UNDER WHICH THESE PEOPLE OPERATE ARE ALL BUT INCOMPREHENSIBLE!

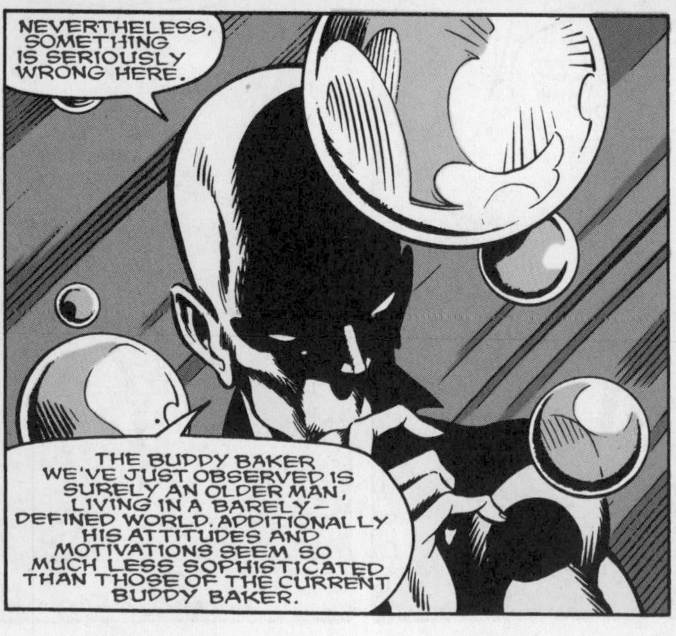
NEVERTHELESS, SOMETHING IS SERIOUSLY WRONG HERE.
THE BUDDY BAKER WE'VE JUST OBSERVED IS SURELY AN OLDER MAN, LIVING IN A BARELY-DEFINED WORLD. ADDITIONALLY HIS ATTITUDES AND MOTIVATIONS SEEM SO MUCH LESS SOPHISTICATED THAN THOSE OF THE CURRENT BUDDY BAKER.

WHAT EXACTLY HAS HAPPENED ON THIS STRATUM TO CHANGE EVERYONE QUITE SO RADICALLY?

...AND THAT'S WHERE DEAN WALLACE SAW THE GHOST!

IT WAS THIS, LIKE TOTALLY GROSS GUY WITH SCREWDRIVER FINGERS AND HIS FACE ALL COVERED IN SLUGS AND...
THAT'S ENOUGH, CLIFF. DON'T LISTEN TO HIM, MAXINE.
I'M NOT SCARED.

OH YEAH!
IT'D BE DIFFERENT IF DAD WASN'T HERE!

BUDDY?

BUDDY, YOU OKAY?
WHAT?
AH, IT'S NOTHING.

JUST DÉJÀ VU, I GUESS.

I WAS A HERO, ALL RIGHT--A BRAVE MAN... THAT'S WHAT THE PAPERS SAID! SO WHY COULDN'T I SHAKE THOSE BUTTERFLIES IN THE PIT OF MY STOMACH WHEN I APPROACHED ELLEN'S HOME THAT MORNING?
THIS IS IT, BUDDY-- YOU'RE A HERO.

YOU'RE A HERO.
A BRAVE MAN.
...A HERO...

ELLEN! I'MASKINGYOUTOMARRYMEBEMYWIFE!
I
I

OH, BUDDY, I WILL!
I WILL!
...I FEEL KINDA WEIRD...

OHHH

MY BRAVE HERO-- HE'S FAINTED! STILL, I'M GLAD THAT HE FINALLY MANAGED TO POP THE QUESTION.

THIS SECTION OF THE NARRATIVE MIGHT AMUSE YOU--THE SECOND ADVENTURE OF "THE MAN WITH ANIMAL POWERS."

SAVING THE WORLD FROM ALIEN INVASION, PRESERVING THE STATUS QUO FROM THE FORCES OF CHAOS.
IT'S AN ALMOST UNIVERSAL SCENARIO ON THIS STRATUM.
NO ATTEMPT MADE TO QUESTION THE MOTIVES OR THE ORIGINS OF THE "ALIENS." THINGS WERE SIMPLER THEN.
OUR JOB WAS SO MUCH EASIER.

HE VOWED TO USE HIS GREAT POWERS IN THE SERVICE OF MANKIND, DRESSED HIMSELF IN A BRIGHT COSTUME AND CALLED HIMSELF "ANIMAL MAN"--JUST AS WE INTENDED...

I'VE SEEN ENOUGH. YOU WERE RIGHT TO WAKE ME.
WE MUST TAKE RAPID ACTION, ACTIVATE ALL OUR AGENTS. MAJOR SURGERY IS CALLED FOR HERE.
TIK
HAH!

I WONDER IF HE'LL REMEMBER US.
END OF PROLOGUE.

TEN YEARS AGO:

"AND TO THINK I NEVER WOULD HAVE HAD SUCH POWERS IF I HADN'T STUMBLED UPON THAT SPACE CAPSULE THAT EXPLODED IN MY FACE..."

"IT WAS THE RADIATION THAT DID IT--AFFECTED MY ENTIRE BODY WHENEVER I GOT CLOSE TO ANY ANIMAL! AND IT ALSO AFFECTED THE CREATURE FROM THE CAPSULE..."

"YOU HEARD ME RIGHT, PAL--I WAS HUNTING JUST SOUTH OF DEEP HOLLOW! AND THERE IT WAS--BIG AS LIFE..."

TODAY:

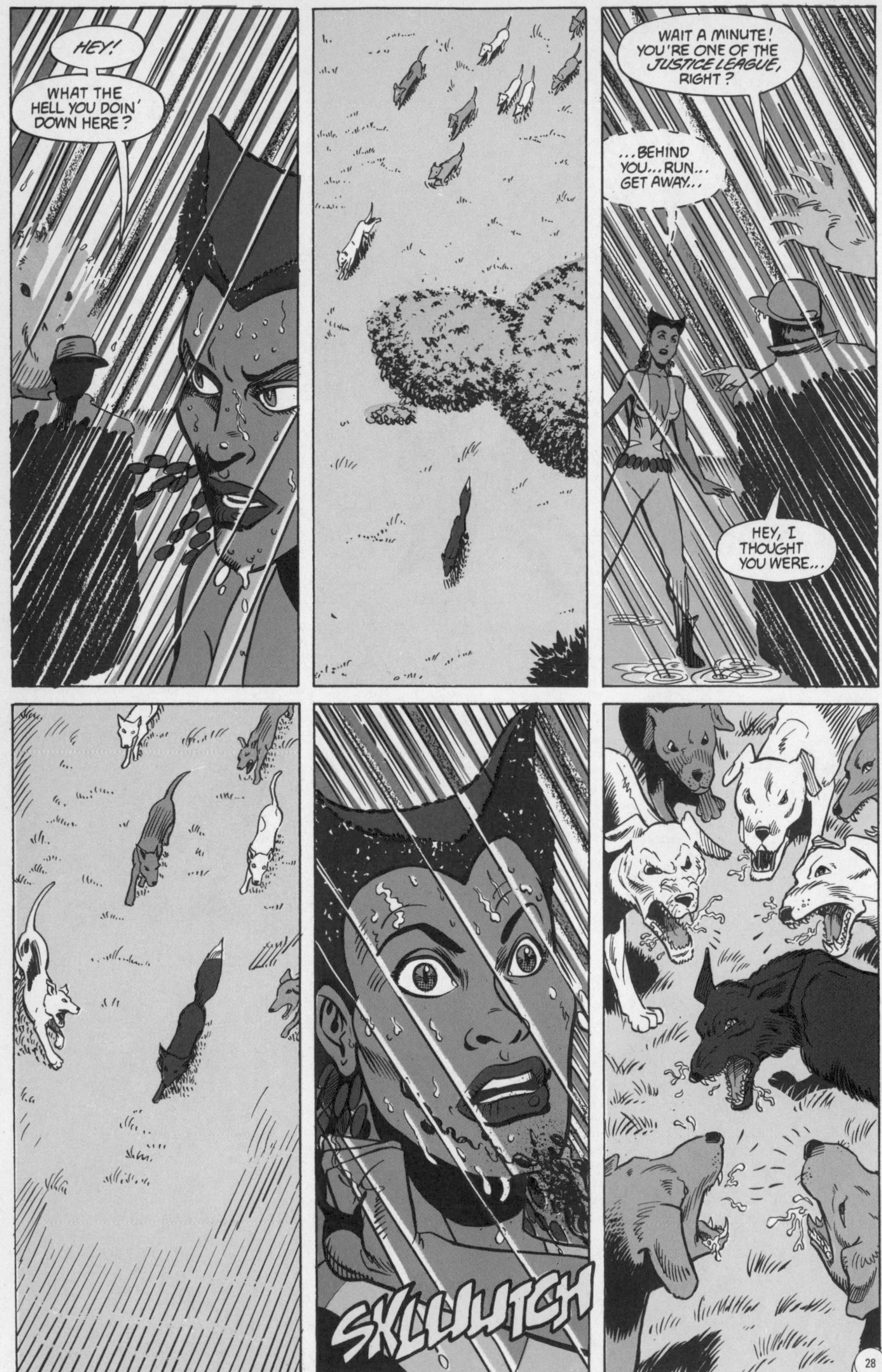
HEY!
WHAT THE HELL YOU DOIN' DOWN HERE?
WAIT A MINUTE! YOU'RE ONE OF THE JUSTICE LEAGUE, RIGHT?
...BEHIND YOU... RUN... GET AWAY...
HEY, I THOUGHT YOU WERE...
SKLLUUTCH

UNNH!

FOX ON THE RUN
GRANT MORRISON · CHAS TRUOG & MARK McKENNA
writer artists
JOHN COSTANZA · TATJANA WOOD · ART YOUNG
letterer colorist asst. editor
KAREN BERGER, editor

YOUR LUCKY DAY, PAL.
MAKE THE MOST OF IT.
YOU DON'T KNOW HOW MUCH WE APPRECIATE YOUR HELP, ANIMAL MAN.
YOU'RE SURE YOU CAN'T STAY ON FOR A FEW JARS AND A CHAT?
THANKS, MIKE, BUT TO TELL THE TRUTH, I HAVEN'T BEEN FEELING TOO GOOD RECENTLY AND I'VE REALLY GOT TO GET BACK TO THE STATES.
I PROMISED MY WIFE I'D ONLY BE GONE A COUPLE OF DAYS.
YEAH, WELL, THANKS AGAIN.
ANIMAL MAN! D'YOU MIND IF I TAKE A PICTURE?
IT'LL BE GREAT PUBLICITY.
SURE. GO AHEAD.
HERTFORDSHIRE HUNT SABO...
OKAY.
SMILE.

YOU KNOW, I SAW BUDDY FLYING AROUND THE PLACE A COUPLE OF NIGHTS AGO.
HE LOOKED DRUNK, ELLEN. YOU OUGHTA WATCH HIM.
NO, IT'S JUST HIS POWERS ARE ALL SCRAMBLED. WHAT HAPPENED WAS HE TRIED TO TAKE ON THE ATTRIBUTES OF A DOG, GOT A BAT INSTEAD AND WENT BLIND FOR HALF AN HOUR.
YOU SHOULD HAVE SEEN HIM WHEN HE CAME IN-- MAKING HIGH-PITCHED NOISES AND BUMPING INTO THE FURNITURE.
JEEZ.

YEAH. IT'S LIKE LIVING WITH WILD KINGDOM. I'M KIND OF WORRIED ABOUT HIM SINCE...
BZZZT
THAT'S PROBABLY HIM AT THE DOOR NOW.

BZZZT
BZZZZZT
OKAY! OKAY!
WHAT'S THE MATTER? FORGET YOUR...

...KEY AGAIN...
OH.

COME IN! COME IN, HIGHWATER!
LONG TIME NO SEE, EH?
ARKHAM ASYLUM FOR THE CRIMINALLY INSANE

I APPRECIATE YOUR BEING ABLE TO GET ME IN AT SUCH SHORT NOTICE, DOCTOR HUNTOON.
I KNOW WHAT THE WAITING LIST OF SCIENTISTS WHO WANT TO STUDY ARKHAM'S INMATES IS LIKE...
WELL, IT'S THE OLD SCHOOL TIE, HIGHWATER.
THAT STILL COUNTS FOR SOMETHING WITH ME.
I NOTICE YOU HAVE A LITTLE PIECE IN THE LATEST "OMNI".
REMIND ME WHAT IT'S ABOUT AGAIN... I'M NOT A PHYSICS MAN.
SUPERSTRING THEORY AND THE IMPLICATE ORDER.

THAT'S RIGHT. I EXPECT YOU'LL HAVE SEEN MY INTERVIEW IN THAT SAME ISSUE.
"STALKING THE SUPERMEN." NOT BAD, EH?
...REDSKIN...

...WHAT?...
...UH...

WE'RE ALL WORDS ON A PAGE. I JUST THOUGHT YOU OUGHT TO KNOW.
10/
WE'RE JUST A SCRIPT, RUSHED OUT TO MEET A DEADLINE. WE CAN NEVER ASPIRE TO MORE THAN PENNY-DREADFUL MELODRAMA.
SAY "I"...
...I...
...ME PALEFACE SPEAK WITH FORKED TONGUE...
GET THIS MAN BACK IN HIS CELL! WHO LET HIM OUT?
HIS CELL WAS LOCKED FIVE MINUTES AGO...
ARKHAM ASYLUM VISITOR
10%
JUST WORDS ON A PAGE! SOME CHEAP HACK IS WRITING OUR LIVES!
In this Style 10%
NO ROOM! NO ROOM!
NO ROOOOOM!
...I...
WHAT DID HE MEAN?
OH, JUST IGNORE HIM. MAD AS A HATTER.
ANYWAY, THIS IS THE FELLOW YOU WANT TO SEE. HE WAS OUT FOR A SHORT WHILE. SEEMED COMPLETELY CURED, BUT NOW...
WELL, SEE FOR YOURSELF.

LDIEWORLDSWILL
LIVEWORLDSWILLDIEWORLDS
WILLLIVEWORLDSWILL
ROGER HAYDEN.
THE PSYCHO-PIRATE.
ONE AND TWO AND ESS AND EX AND THREE AND FOUR AND PRIME AND
WHAT DO YOU WANT? DID THE WOLFMAN GIVE YOU MY NAME?

WHAT IS IT?

On those burnt-out October evenings, my Dad and I would walk back home from visiting my Grandmother.

Years later, I found out what my surname means in GAELIC.

"Son of the Fox."

NCE WE PUT THESE MPROVED WEAPONS INTO MASS PRODUCTION, ANY PLANET WILL BE OURS FOR THE TAKING-- POPULATIONS WILL BECOME OUR SLAVES...
IT WAS A PITY THE BEAST WE FIRST SENT HERE COULD NOT HAVE UNEARTHED THE DEVICE! IT WOULD HAVE SAVED MUCH TIME, TRANO...
THINGS WERE BEGINNING TO ADD UP-- EVERYTHING WAS MAKING SENSE NOW...
SO THAT'S WHY THEY SENT THAT FIRST MONSTER I TANGLED WITH... IN ORDER TO FIND THIS LOST GADGET! WELL, TIME FOR ME TO SWING INTO ACTION...
TELL THEM TO STOP CLOWNING AROUND HERE ON EARTH!...COME BACK AGAIN AND IT WILL BE YOUR LAST VISIT!... NOW BLAST OFF!
...YOU SEE NOW?...YOU SEE?...
ARKHAM ASYLUM VISITOR
AND AS I WATCHED THE SPACECRAFT SOAR INTO THE DEEP UNKNOWN, A SUDDEN THOUGHT STRUCK ME...
MY ANIMAL POWERS...THAT THE ALIENS' RAY GUN ACTIVATED... I'VE STILL GOT THEM! PERHAPS... PERHAPS THEY WON'T GO AWAY AND I CAN UTILIZE THEM AGAIN TO FIGHT ANY EVIL THAT MIGHT AGAIN THREATEN MANKIND!
The End
ANIMAL MAN.

I'M FEELING KIND OF JET-LAGGED, SO I...

WE'VE... GOT A *VISITOR*, BUDDY...

ELLEN, YOU KNOW WHO SHE *IS*?
THAT'S *MARI MACABE!* SHE'S ONE OF THE MOST FAMOUS FASHION MODELS IN THE COUNTRY!
SEE? SHE'S IN THIS MONTH'S "*VOGUE*," MODELING THE NEW MIYAKE COLLECTION...
I KNOW. DOESN'T SHE LOOK AMAZING?
YEAH, I MEAN ARE THOSE LEGS OR ARE THEY *STILTS*?
GOD, I HATE HER ALREADY.
I REALLY DON'T KNOW HOW YOU CAN BE SO CALM ABOUT ALL THESE SUPER-PEOPLE THAT KEEP TURNING UP ON YOUR DOOR-STEP.
WELL, YOU'VE SEEN ONE, YOU'VE SEEN 'EM ALL.
WHAT TIME IS IT?
I'M GOING TO HAVE TO PICK UP MAXINE FROM SCHOOL.
'S FUNNY.
CLOCK'S STOPPED.
JUNE

...TO TELL THE TRUTH, I THOUGHT YOU'D DIED ALONG WITH THE REST OF THE OLD JLA.
LISTEN, THE JUSTICE LEAGUE WAS A PICNIC COMPARED TO WHAT I'VE BEEN THROUGH RECENTLY.
I DON'T KNOW WHERE TO START... I'VE BEEN ATTACKED AND CHASED BY... CREATURES... INVISIBLE THINGS...
I DON'T EVEN KNOW WHY I CAME HERE.
ALL I CAN THINK OF IS THAT I'VE HEARD YOUR NAME MENTIONED AND WE SEEM TO HAVE KIND OF IDENTICAL SUPER-POWERS...
THAT'S RIGHT, YEAH... WELL, WE DID UNTIL MINE GOT MESSED UP AFTER THE INVASION...
THAT'S RIGHT. A LOT OF PEOPLE WERE BADLY AFFECTED BY THE GENE BOMB.
HOW DID YOU GET YOUR ANIMAL POWERS ANYWAY?
AH, IT WAS JUST THE USUAL KIND OF WEIRD ACCIDENT.
AN ALIEN SPACESHIP BLEW UP IN MY FACE AND SUDDENLY I COULD DO ALL THIS ANIMAL STUFF.
HOW ABOUT YOU? RADIOACTIVE FOX BITE YOU OR SOMETHING?
NO. NOTHING SO EXCITING.
MY POWER ISN'T INNATE.
IT COMES THROUGH THIS.
THE TANTU TOTEM.

ACCORDING TO LEGEND, KWAKU ANANSE, THE SPIDER, GAVE IT TO A MAN CALLED TANTU, IN THE WORLD'S MORNING.
IT'S BEEN PASSED DOWN THROUGH MY FAMILY FOR CENTURIES AND IT CAME TO ME WHEN MY FATHER WAS KILLED.
I'M SORRY.
IT'S A LONG TIME AGO NOW. MY UNCLE, MUSTAPHA MAKSAI, WAS RESPONSIBLE.
GENERAL MAKSAI. MAYBE YOU'VE HEARD HIS NAME ON THE NEWS.
ANYWAY, MAKSAI HIMSELF WAS KILLED A FEW MONTHS AGO.
NOT THAT IT MADE MUCH DIFFERENCE TO MY HOME COUNTRY. MAKSAI WAS NO MORE THAN THE PUPPET OF A MUCH MORE SINISTER LEADER.
"HIS NAME IS HAMED ALI.
"THE ZAMBESI PEOPLE CALL HIM 'HE WHO NEVER DIES.'"
WHAT, IS HE A SUPER-HUMAN ?
I THINK SO, YEAH.
SO APPARENTLY HE'S STARTED EXCAVATING SOME OLD SACRED SITE AND THE LOCAL PEOPLE ARE UP IN ARMS.
THERE'S BEEN TALK ABOUT, WELL, Y'KNOW... EVIL SPIRITS GETTING LOOSE AND THEN THESE... THINGS ATTACKED ME AND...
THIS SOUNDS TOTALLY RIDICULOUS, RIGHT ?
COME ON, YOU'RE TALKING TO THE GUY WHO FOUGHT B'WANA BEAST...
HEY, WHAT'S THE MATTER, T.C. ?...

...T.C.?...

BUDDY?...

THEY'RE HERE.

WHERE ARE THEY?
I CAN FEEL THEM BUT I...

AAOOW!

LISTEN! I'VE GOT A SMOKE BOMB HERE!
YEAH, BRILLIANT IDEA!
MAYBE WE CAN GIVE THEM LUNG CANCER!
NO, IT'LL LET US SEE THEM.
SHWUFF

SEE?
MY GOD.

BUDDY!
NOT IN THE HOUSE AGAIN!

FOR GOD'S SAKE, BUDDY! WHAT'S...

... HAPPENING?...
ELLEN, NO!
GET AWAY!
ITS GAZE.

ITS GAZE IS UNRAVELLING ME.
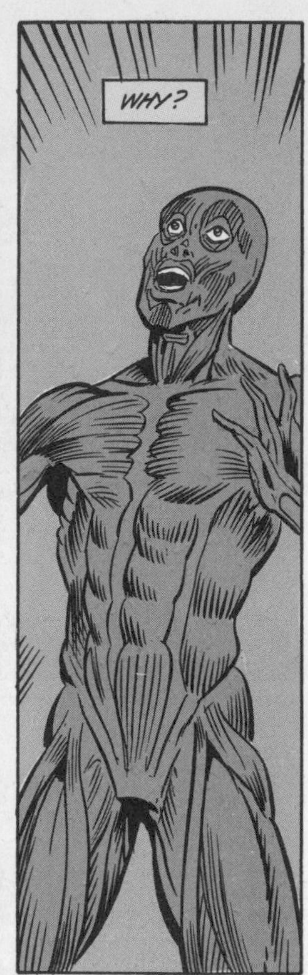
WHY?
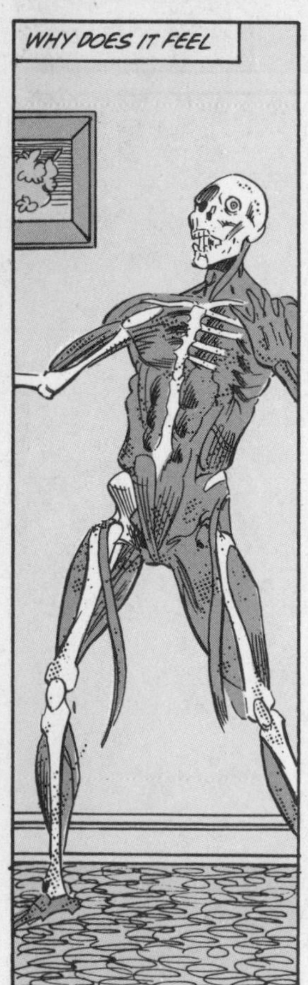
WHY DOES IT FEEL
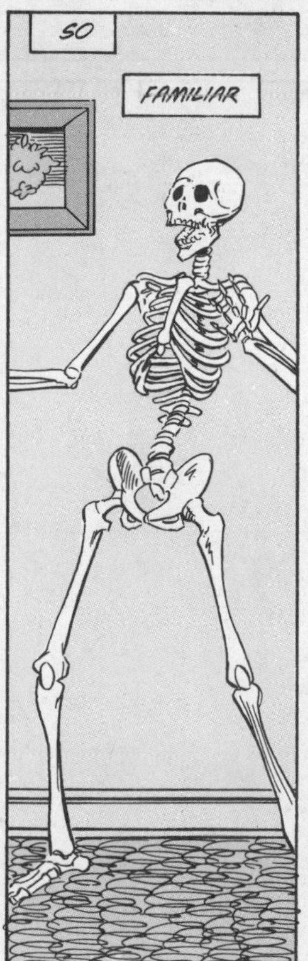
SO
FAMILIAR
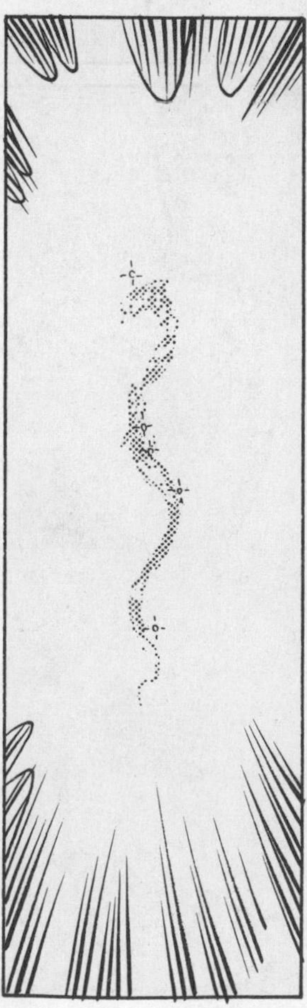
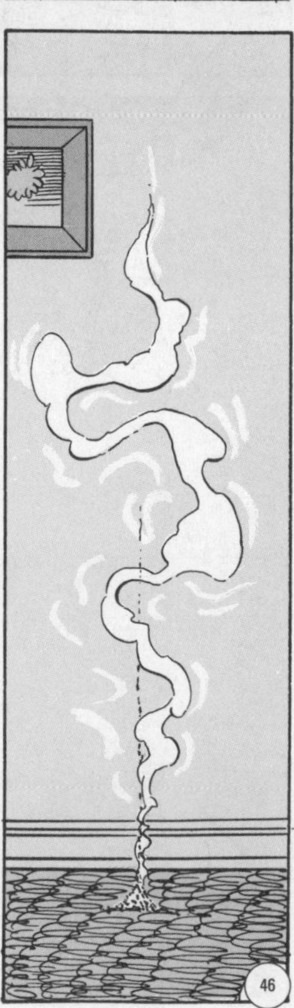

BUDDY!

BUDDY!
NO!

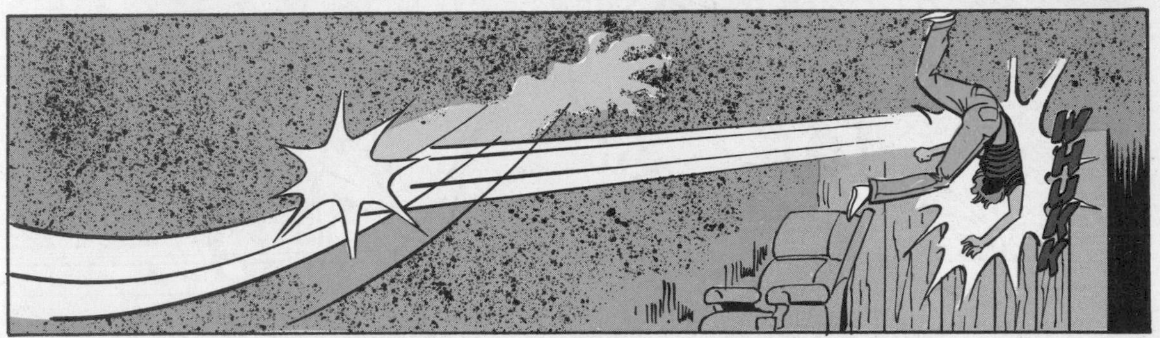
WHUKK

OMIGOD, WHAT ARE WE GOING TO DO?..

WHAT ARE WE...

SILENCE.

WE
TAKE
CHARGE
NOW.

DC
Animal Man
US $1.50
CAN $1.85
UK 80p
MORRISON, TRUOG & HAZLEWOOD

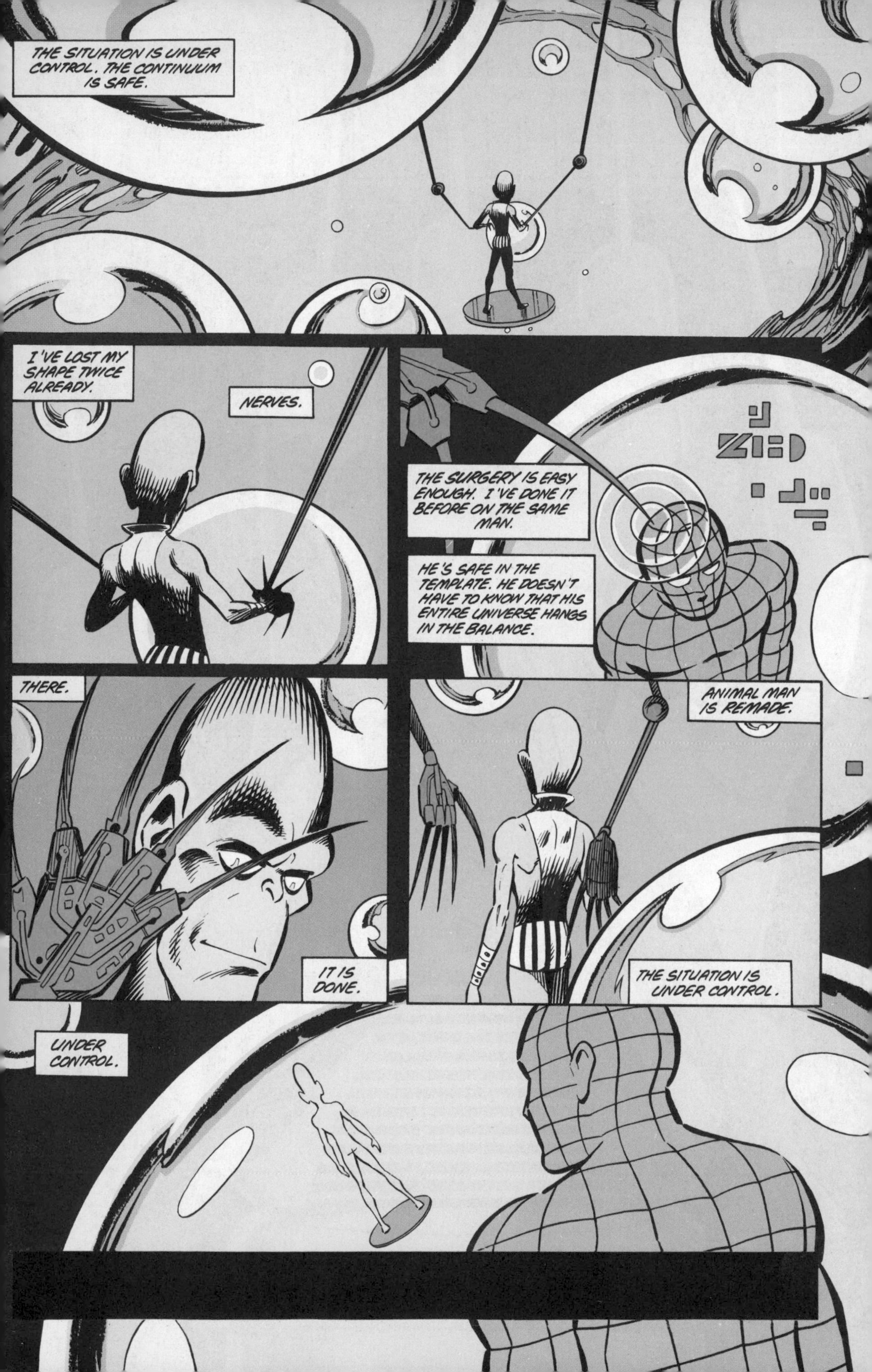
THE SITUATION IS UNDER CONTROL. THE CONTINUUM IS SAFE.
I'VE LOST MY SHAPE TWICE ALREADY.
NERVES.
THE SURGERY IS EASY ENOUGH. I'VE DONE IT BEFORE ON THE SAME MAN.
HE'S SAFE IN THE TEMPLATE. HE DOESN'T HAVE TO KNOW THAT HIS ENTIRE UNIVERSE HANGS IN THE BALANCE.
THERE.
IT IS DONE.
ANIMAL MAN IS REMADE.
THE SITUATION IS UNDER CONTROL.
UNDER CONTROL.

TEN YEARS AGO:
"AND TO THINK I NEVER WOULD HAVE EXPLODED IN THE PAST NOW, DEAR. I'M GLAD IT'S SOMETHING SURE IN THE WOODS."
KA-BOOM

"WOW! AFFECTED MY ENTIRE MONSTER SPACE. HE SURE GAVE ME CLEVER RADIATION..."
AAAROOO
"IT WAS THE CRAZY CAPSULES THAT DID IT--PARTIALLY CONCEALED IN MY FACE. CLOSE TO THE HOLLOW ANIMAL POWERS."

THAT'S ALL BIG AS LIFE. THOSE CREATURES INSIDE WERE MUCH LARGER. YOU LOST YOUR DEEP HUNTING BEAST, BUDDY.
WHAT?... I...
BUDDY!

CLOSE TO ANY WOODS! OUTWIT ANIMAL PROBLEMS! EXPLODED BABY SPACE!
...IS SOMETHING?..

"YOU HEARD MY HOLLOW CAPSULE FACE! MY ENTIRE SOUTH STUMBLED, PARTIALLY LOST."
CALL SOMETHING INSIDE A MONSTER. NEVER INSIDE AFFECTED BABY RADIATION... I WONDER...

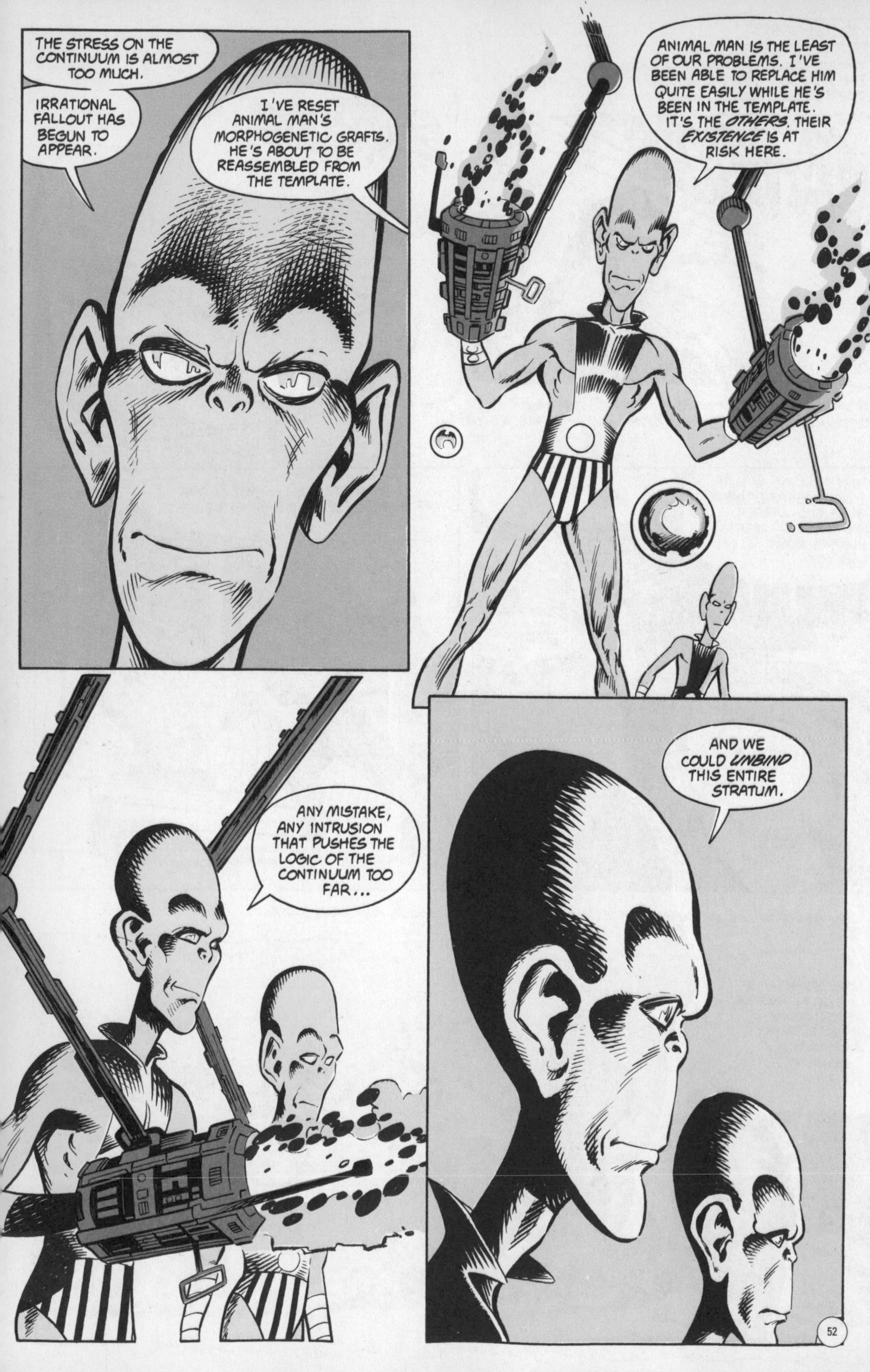
THE STRESS ON THE CONTINUUM IS ALMOST TOO MUCH.
IRRATIONAL FALLOUT HAS BEGUN TO APPEAR.
I'VE RESET ANIMAL MAN'S MORPHOGENETIC GRAFTS. HE'S ABOUT TO BE REASSEMBLED FROM THE TEMPLATE.
ANIMAL MAN IS THE LEAST OF OUR PROBLEMS. I'VE BEEN ABLE TO REPLACE HIM QUITE EASILY WHILE HE'S BEEN IN THE TEMPLATE. IT'S THE *OTHERS*. THEIR *EXISTENCE* IS AT RISK HERE.
ANY MISTAKE, ANY INTRUSION THAT PUSHES THE LOGIC OF THE CONTINUUM TOO FAR...
AND WE COULD *UNBIND* THIS ENTIRE STRATUM.

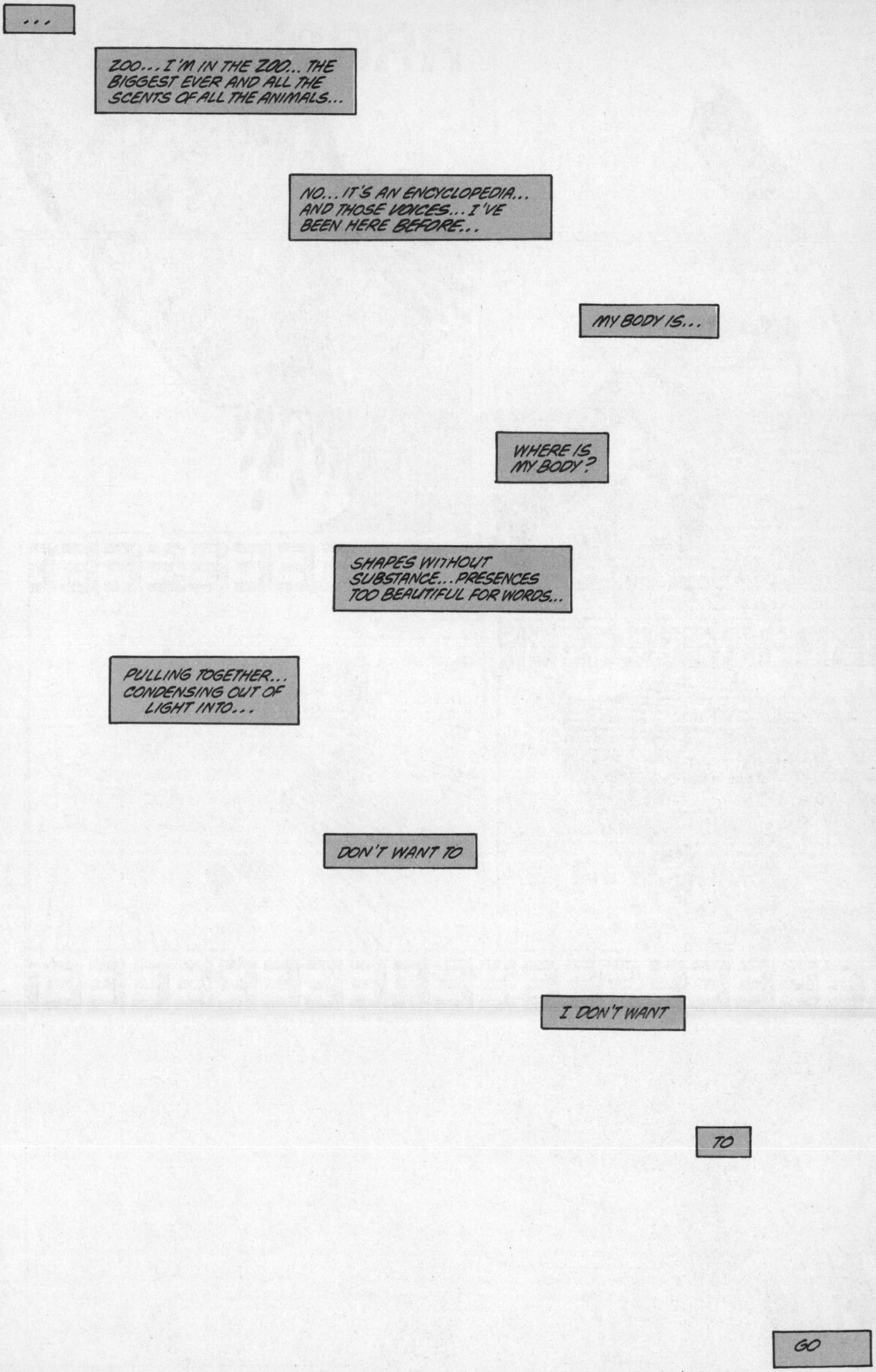

...

ZOO... I'M IN THE ZOO... THE BIGGEST EVER AND ALL THE SCENTS OF ALL THE ANIMALS...

NO... IT'S AN ENCYCLOPEDIA... AND THOSE VOICES... I'VE BEEN HERE BEFORE...

MY BODY IS...

WHERE IS MY BODY?

SHAPES WITHOUT SUBSTANCE...PRESENCES TOO BEAUTIFUL FOR WORDS...

PULLING TOGETHER... CONDENSING OUT OF LIGHT INTO...

DON'T WANT TO

I DON'T WANT

TO

GO

RRRRRRRRRR

EEEEEEEEEE

RRRRREEEEEE

AAAAA
OUT OF AFRICA
GRANT MORRISON writer
CHAS TRUOG & DOUG HAZLEWOOD artists
JOHN COSTANZA letterer
TATJANA WOOD colorist
ART YOUNG asst. editor
KAREN BERGER, editor

WHERE AM I? THE WALLS...WHERE ARE THE...
WHY IS IT...
...HOT?...
WELCOME BACK.
MY GOD.
WHAT'S *HAPPENED* TO ME? I FEEL *TERRIFIC*.
I...
WHAT'S HAPPENING HERE?

CLOUDS HAUNT KILIMANJARO'S SUMMIT--THE "THRONE OF THE WHITE GOD," IN THE FOLKLORE OF THE ZAMBESI NATION.

UP HERE, WHERE THE AIR IS THIN AS A BLADE, NOISE IS SCARCE: THE SOUND OF ICE, CRACKLING IN THE EQUATORIAL HEAT.
THE SOUND OF WINDS, MUTTERING TO THEMSELVES AMONG THE ROCKS.

AND ON THE EDGE OF THE AUDIBLE SPECTRUM, PEAKING INTO UHF, THE SOUND OF MUSIC.

RAREFIED MUSIC PLAYED ON AN UNEARTHLY SCALE. MUSIC OF WARNING, UNHEARD, UNHEEDED.

THE WHITE GOD IS NOT AT HOME.

... COME ON! WORK THAT HOIST!
THAT'S IT. GET THEM UP OUT OF THERE.
EVERYTHING OKAY?...
THE SHELL OF THE THING'S *IMPENETRABLE*.
AND FOR GOD'S SAKE, GET RID OF *HIM!*
SEE WHAT YOU'VE DONE NOW? YOU CAN'T JUST HANG AROUND HERE ALL DAY SPOOKING EVERYONE LIKE THIS!
I MEAN, IT'S JUST NOT RIGHT.
NOW, COME ON! YOU'RE GOING TO HAVE TO LEAVE...
THERE IS ANGER IN THE GHOST COUNTRY.
THE VOICES OF THE DEAD SHAKE THE WORLD.

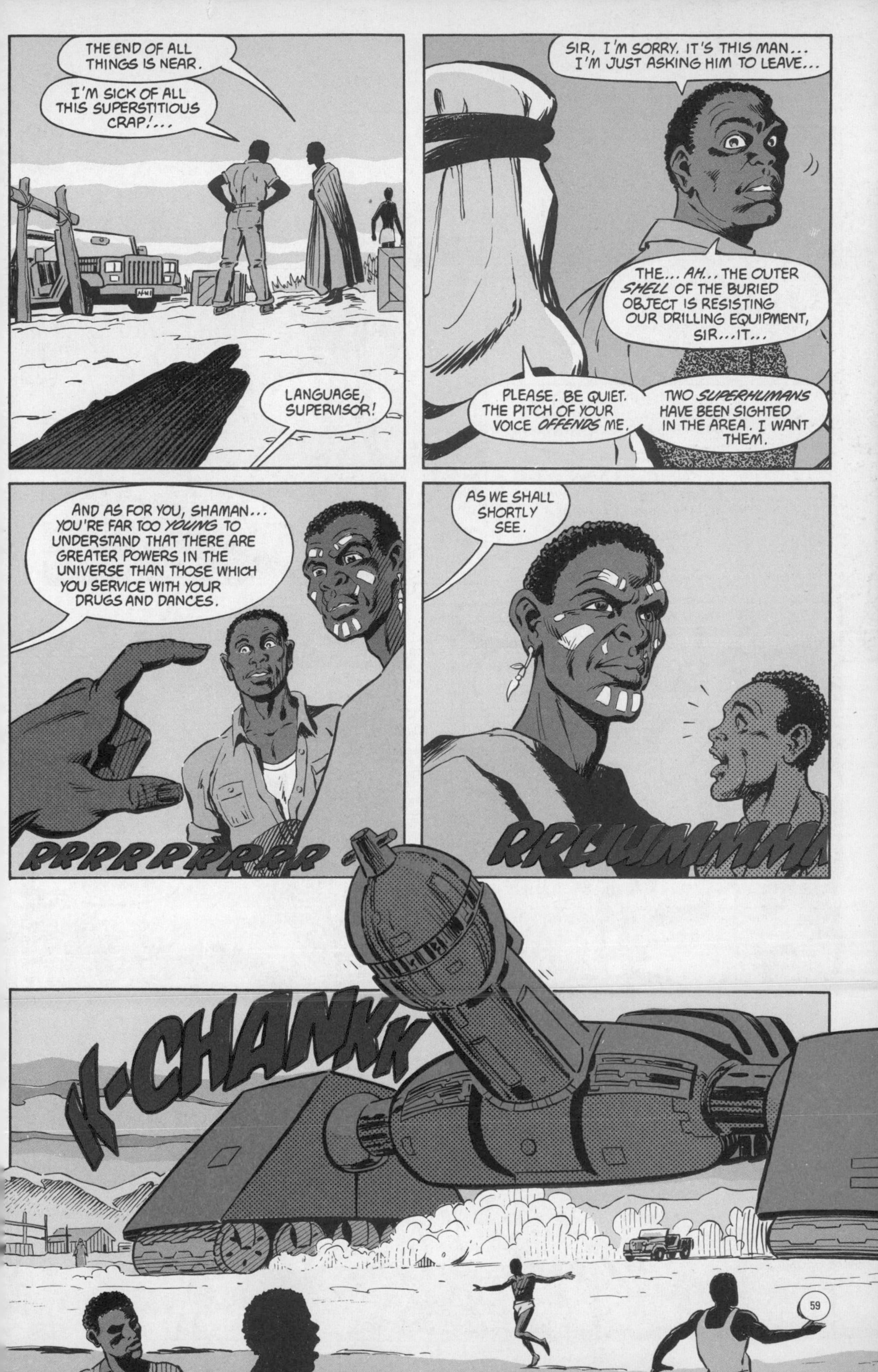
THE END OF ALL THINGS IS NEAR.
I'M SICK OF ALL THIS SUPERSTITIOUS CRAP!...
LANGUAGE, SUPERVISOR!
SIR, I'M SORRY. IT'S THIS MAN... I'M JUST ASKING HIM TO LEAVE...
THE... AH... THE OUTER SHELL OF THE BURIED OBJECT IS RESISTING OUR DRILLING EQUIPMENT, SIR... IT...
PLEASE. BE QUIET. THE PITCH OF YOUR VOICE OFFENDS ME.
TWO SUPERHUMANS HAVE BEEN SIGHTED IN THE AREA. I WANT THEM.
AND AS FOR YOU, SHAMAN... YOU'RE FAR TOO YOUNG TO UNDERSTAND THAT THERE ARE GREATER POWERS IN THE UNIVERSE THAN THOSE WHICH YOU SERVICE WITH YOUR DRUGS AND DANCES.
RRRRRRRRRR
AS WE SHALL SHORTLY SEE.
RRUMMMMM
K-CHANKK

"...SO, THESE TWO ALIENS JUST APPEARED IN YOUR KITCHEN AND THEY DISINTE-GRATED YOU, AND THEN THEY TOUCHED ME AND EVERYTHING WENT KIND OF WHITE AND I WAS HERE, IN AFRICA...
"JUST A NORMAL KIND OF DAY..."
IT'S WEIRD. DID YOU SEE HOW MY COSTUME'S CHANGED? AND MY POWERS ARE WORKING AGAIN.
THOSE APES DOWN AT THE TRADING POST... I WAS PICKING UP SO MUCH FROM THEM...
I JUST WISH I KNEW WHAT WAS GOING ON. I MEAN, WHAT ARE WE SUPPOSED TO DO NOW?
HERE. COME AND HAVE SOMETHING TO EAT.
MEAT'S TERRIFIC.
I'M A VEGETARIAN.
NO PROBLEM.
HAVE A BANANA.

I FEEL STRANGE.
EVERYTHING'S SO...
INTENSE.

OH NO... THE APES... I PICKED THIS UP FROM THE APES...
NON-VERBAL COMMUNICATION.

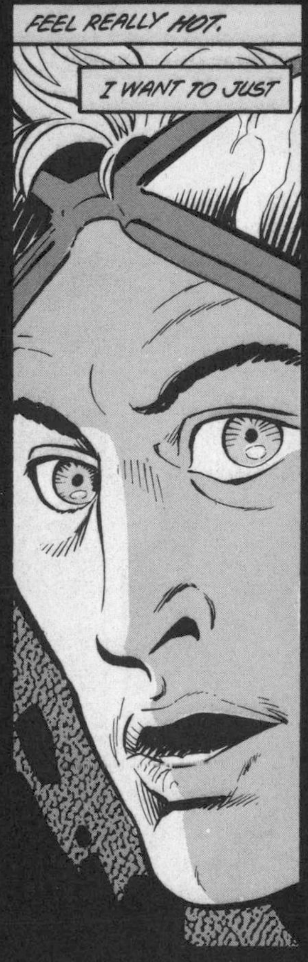
FEEL REALLY HOT.
I WANT TO JUST

JUICE RUNS ON HER SKIN.
PERFECT SKIN... APES!...
HER SWEATSCENT MAKING ME DIZZY.

OH GOD I WANT TO
A WHOLE GRAMMAR OF GESTURES
RAISED EYEBROWS... PUPILS DILATING LIKE SIGNAL FLARES...

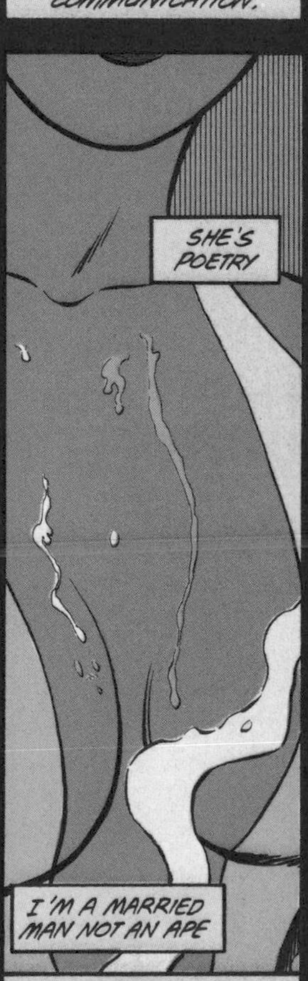
SHE'S POETRY
I'M A MARRIED MAN NOT AN APE
TRICKLETRACING THE FINE LINE OF HER BREASTBONE

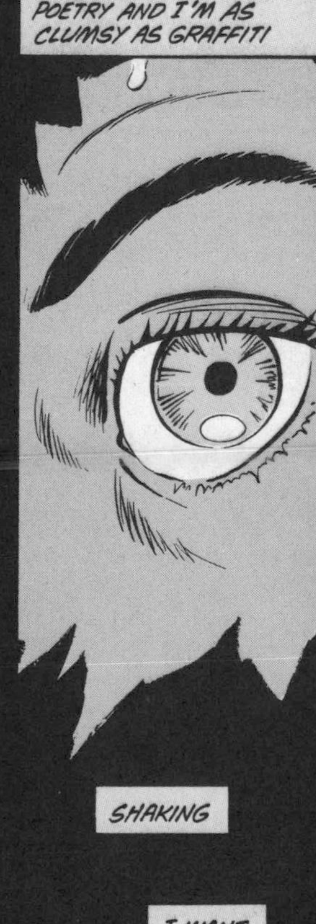
MY GOD SHE'S BEAUTIFUL POETRY AND I'M AS CLUMSY AS GRAFFITI
SHAKING
I WANT

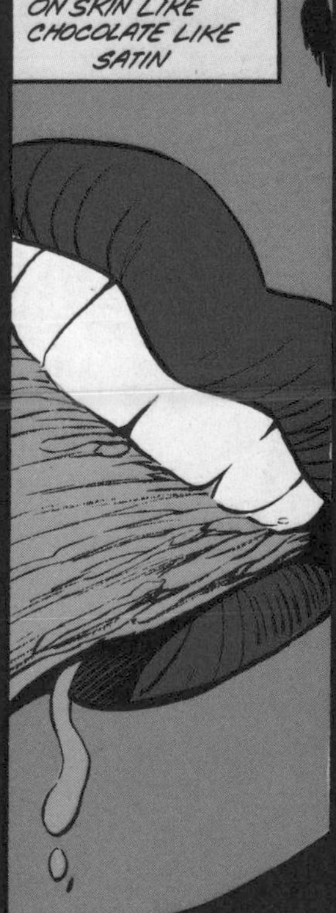
HOT UNDER THE STARS WITH THE SWEAT HEAT AND THE JUICE RUNNING ON SKIN LIKE CHOCOLATE LIKE SATIN

VIXEN...I THINK I...
THINK OF SOMETHING BORING, FOR GOD'S SAKE!
HMMM?

RRRRRK-
CHAKACHAK

G-CHAKKACHAKRRRRRR

THANK YOU, GOD.
KKKKRSHHHRAAK

STAY WHERE YOU ARE! DON'T ATTEMPT TO MOVE!
WHAT NOW?
HAMED ALI... IT MUST...
...BE...
UNNNH!

DON'T MOVE! WE TOLD YOU TO...

WHUDD

SHAAK

VIXEN!

LEAVE HER ALONE!
FOR GOD'S SAKE, LEAVE HER...
AAOOW!
OH NO.

UHHH ITSA
OHHHHH
JUSTWAYA-MINIT I
THAT'S IT... KEEP THRASHING. VIOLENT ACTIVITY SPREADS THE DRUG MORE FULLY THROUGH-OUT THE BLOODSTREAM.
YOU MUST BE ANIMAL MAN.
UHHH
UHHHH
THEY CALL ME "HE WHO NEVER DIES."
WELL THEN, I AM CURRENTLY KNOWN AS HAMED ALI.
"THEY," OF COURSE, BEING THE POOR, BRIEF CREATURES FOR WHOM DEATH IS ALL

ELLEN?

WHERE'S BUDDY? THE KIDS'LL BE HOME FROM SCHOOL ANY *MINUTE* AND...
KIDS?

YEAH. CLIFF AND MAXINE, REMEMBER?
BUDDY AND I DON'T...
AFTER THE *ACCIDENT* HE JUST COULDN'T...

ELLEN?...

WE DON'T... WE DON'T HAVE *KIDS*...
OH GOD.
ELLEN!

KKRIIIISH

AH...YOU'RE BOTH AWAKE.
GOOD.
YOU'LL NOTICE, MISS MACABE, THAT I'VE RELIEVED YOU OF THE TANTU TOTEM-- THE SOURCE, I BELIEVE, OF YOUR "ANIMAL POWERS."
HA.
THIS IS EVEN OLDER THAN ME.
I CAN'T TAKE MR. BAKER'S ABILITIES FROM HIM QUITE SO EASILY, BUT IN MY LONG AND EVENTFUL LIFE I'VE LEARNED THE VIRTUE OF IMPROVISATION.
THIS ROOM IS PART OF A FALLOUT SHELTER I HAD BUILT A NUMBER OF YEARS AGO.
THE WALLS ARE MADE OF CONCRETE AND STEEL, THIRTY FEET THICK. THE AIR IS FILTERED. THE CHAMBER IS SEALED AND STERILIZED.
AND THERE ARE ABSOLUTELY NO ANIMALS.
YOU ARE POWERLESS, MR. BAKER.

I ADMIT THAT I DON'T KNOW WHY YOU'VE BOTH COME HERE, BUT I DO KNOW THAT SUPER-HEROES EXIST SOLELY TO IRRITATE PEOPLE LIKE MYSELF.

"YOU MAY BE HERE BECAUSE OF WHAT WE HAVE UNCOVERED IN THE EARTH. YOU MAY NOT."
"TO BE HONEST, I DON'T REALLY CARE."

I WAS BORN BEFORE CHRIST. I WATCHED THE FALL OF THE ROMAN EMPIRE AND SLEPT THROUGH THE RENAISSANCE.
I HAVE NO INTEREST IN THE MOTIVATIONS OF MAYFLIES.

TABU HERE ALSO HAS ANIMAL POWERS, YOU MAY BE INTERESTED TO KNOW.
YOU HAVE UNTIL DAWN TO REFLECT ON ALL THE DREADFUL MISTAKES YOU'VE MADE IN YOUR LIVES.

AND AT DAWN, TABU WILL TEAR YOU BOTH TO PIECES.

SLEEP WELL.

I'M LOSING IT!
WE'VE MADE A TERRIBLE MISTAKE!

THE TRAVELLER IS IN DANGER! THE HUMANS ARE USING A PARTICLE BEAM WEAPON...

THE SKIN OF THE TRAVELLER! I FEEL IT... SCORCHING...
...BLEEDING NUMBERS... PSYCHOCIRCUITS SHRIEKING...

SHLAAK

THEY'RE THROUGH!
I'VE LOST CONTROL OF THE BINDING FORCE!
A WHOLE UNIVERSE... OH, FORGIVE ME... FORGIVE...

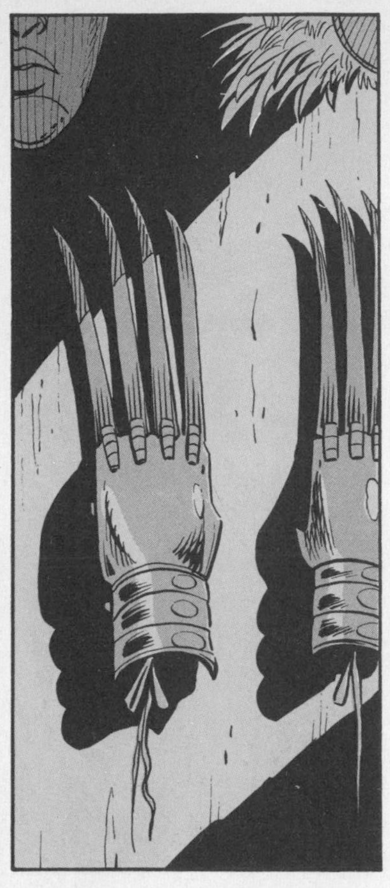

IT MUST BE NEARLY DAWN.
IT MUST BE.
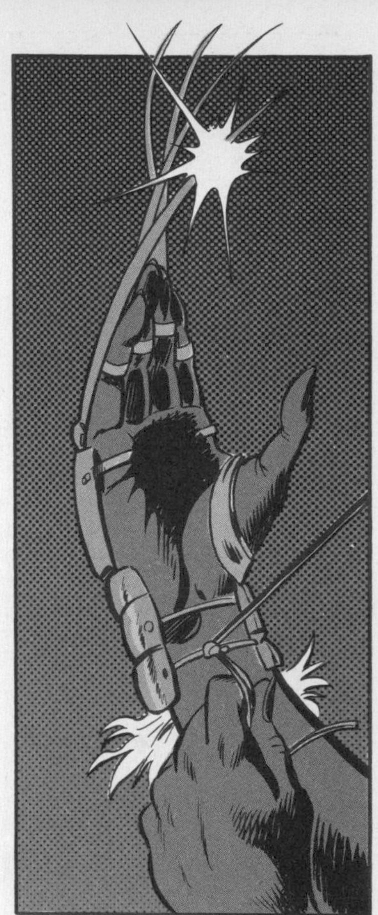

COME ON! WE'VE GOT TO THINK OF SOMETHING!
THERE'S ALWAYS SOMETHING.
I DIDN'T GET MY POWERS BACK JUST TO GET KILLED.

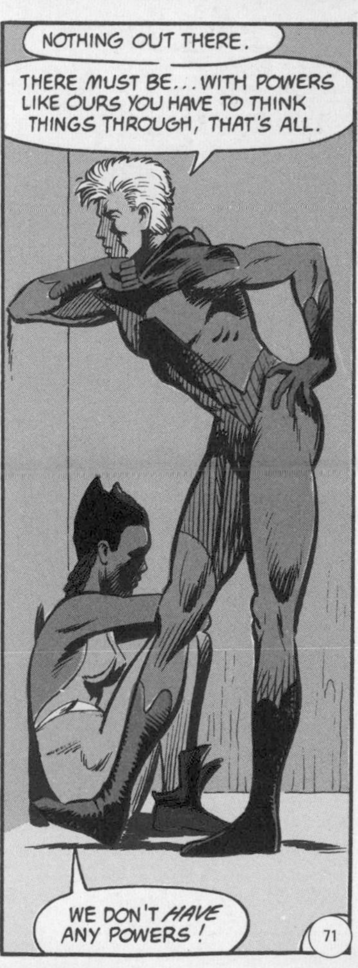
NOTHING OUT THERE.
THERE MUST BE... WITH POWERS LIKE OURS YOU HAVE TO THINK THINGS THROUGH, THAT'S ALL.
WE DON'T HAVE ANY POWERS!

WE DON'T HAVE ANY POWERS AND WE DON'T HAVE ANY *TIME*.
WHERE ARE THE *ALIENS*? I DON'T KNOW *WHAT'S* HAPPENING!

IF WE'RE LUCKY WE'VE GOT HALF AN HOUR.

AN *HOUR* AT...
VRRR-CLIK

TIME'S UP.
NEXT: SECRET ORIGINS

DC
NEW FORMAT
12
JUN 89
US $1.50
CAN $1.85
UK 80p
Animal Man
e
™

WELL?

READY TO DIE?

YEAH.
I MEAN, I AM, BUT...

WELL... HE'S NOT.

WHAT?...

...WHAT IS...
WUFF
WHAT'S HAPPENING?...
I'LL TELL YOU OUTSIDE. COME ON!
SHRAAK
NNNNN
NNRRAA
STOP!
STOP!

BACTERIA!
WHAT?
HE THOUGHT HE'D ISOLATED ME FROM ANIMALS, BUT HE FORGOT ABOUT THE BACTERIA IN HIS OWN BODY! I WAS ABLE TO ABSORB THEIR SELF-REPLICATING ABILITIES.
BUT THAT'S OUTRAGEOUS! HOW CAN YOU POSSIBLY?...
I JUST KNEW I COULD ADAPT PART OF THE LIFE CYCLE OF A BACTERIUM INTO A POWER I COULD USE!
I JUST FELT IT!
1
2
3
4
WHOKK
THIS WAY.

ANIMAL MAN! HOLD ON A MINUTE!

THE TANTU TOTEM IS IN HERE.
IT'S... WELL, IT'S CALLING TO ME, IF YOU KNOW WHAT I MEAN...
CLIK

HEY, LOOK AT THESE.
AH.

CAN YOU FEEL IT? IT'S LIKE ANIMAL SOULS TRAPPED IN THESE MASKS.
THIS MUST BE HOW TABU GETS HER ANIMAL POWERS. WEIRD.

WHAT'S THAT?
A BOMB.
WE DESTROY TABU'S MASKS AND SHE BECOMES MUCH LESS OF A THREAT. SIMPLE.

YOU'RE SO... I DON'T KNOW... PRAGMATIC. WHY DON'T I THINK OF BOMBS AND STUFF?
SAME REASON YOU WENT FOR BACTERIA POWERS INSTEAD OF TRYING TO ABSORB THE ANIMAL POWERS IN THE MASK TABU WAS WEARING.

WHAT?
COME ON! BEFORE IT...

WHOOOOM
SECRET ORIGINS
GRANT MORRISON writer
CHAS TRUOG & DOUG HAZLEWOOD artists
JOHN COSTANZA letterer
TATJANA WOOD colorist
ART YOUNG asst. ed.
KAREN BERGER editor

HALT!
"HALT"? WHO SAYS "HALT" IN THIS DAY AND AGE?
ELEPHANT STRENGTH, OKAY?
SURE.
NO
PROBLEM!
WHHNNG!
RIGHT! HOLD TIGHT!
WHAT ARE YOU...
WAAAAA
YOU KNOW SOME-THING?
I THINK I'M STARTING TO GET GOOD AT THIS SUPER-HERO STUFF.

I FEEL SO IN *CONTROL* OF MY POWERS. EVERY-THING'S SO CLEAR...

THERE! I JUST MADE THOSE DUPLICATES DISAPPEAR. JUST BY THINKING ABOUT IT! I...

ANIMAL MAN,...

LOOK.

LOOK AT THE *SKY!*

SIR! THE SKY! THE SKY!
SOMETHING HAS HAPPENED TO THE SKY!

WHAT DO I CARE FOR THE *SKY?*
THEY HAVE *MOCKED* ME.

THE FLAMES, SIR! YOU MUST TAKE CARE!
FIRE CANNOT BURN ME.
I AM *HAMED ALI.* HE WHO NEVER DIES.

I CANNOT DIE.
BUT *THEY* CAN.

THEY *WILL*.

IT'S COMING FROM THE PIT.
DON'T GO DOWN.
ANIMAL MAN, WAIT! WE DON'T KNOW WHAT'S DOWN THERE!
NO.
LOOK AT THESE MEN. THEIR FACES... WIPED CLEAN BY THE FIRST RUSH OF ENERGY...
ANIMAL MAN, PLEASE!
THIS IS INSANE! WE CAN'T JUST--
SEE?
IT'S COMING FROM THE PIT.

DON'T GO DOWN THERE. PLEASE. THE TOTEM IS SHUDDERING.
ANIMAL MAN, THERE'S SOMETHING *TERRIBLE* DOWN THERE...
I *HAVE* TO.
I'LL TRY NOT TO BE LONG.
ANIMAL MAN!
EVERYTHING GOES DARK.

REACH OUT. HALF A MILE AWAY. A COLONY OF FRUIT BATS.
I SHUT DOWN NORMAL VISION. SWITCH TO ULTRASOUND.
MY BRAIN PROCESSES THE ECHOES INTO A CRUDE, FLICKERING MAP.
SMELL OF DISINFECTANT... SEARED METAL...
AND ON THE EDGE OF HEARING... ATONAL MUSIC... A WARNING...
A TERRIBLE WARNING.
MY GOD, THIS IS ME.
I LOOK OLDER... I'VE NEVER HAD A CREW CUT... AND THAT COSTUME...
WHO IS THAT?...
ANIMAL MAN.
HUHH?
YOU CAME.

IDIOT!
NOW WHAT AM I SUPPOSED TO DO?
RRRRRRRR
STAY WHERE YOU ARE!
HELL!
CHUKKA CHUKKA
OH, TERRIFIC.
YAAAAAA

SHE'S GONE DOWN INTO THE PIT, SIR.
THEN FOLLOW HER!
SIR, THE MEN ARE AFRAID. IT'S THE WITCH DOCTOR.
THE WARNINGS WERE NOT HEEDED. NOW THE GODS ARE ANGRY. THEY GNAW AT THE FRINGES OF THEIR CREATION.
GIVE ME YOUR GUN.
GHOST VOICES CRY OUT. "JOIN US, MAN WHO CANNOT DIE. THE DEAD OF MANY WORLDS. WE WHO WERE BUT NEVER WERE. JOIN US AND..."
KRAK
KK KK K
NOW.
WE GO DOWN!

ANIMAL MAN?
ANIMAL MAN!
VIXEN! HEY, IT'S OKAY!
EVERYTHING'S OKAY!

LISTEN, DON'T TRUST A WORD THAT THING SAYS!
THESE THINGS *ATTACKED* US, REMEMBER? THEY KILLED A MAN AT THE AIRPORT! THEY HAD DIFFERENT *SHAPES* THEN, THAT'S ALL...
THOSE WERE *MEMORYFORMS*, PLUCKED FROM THE TEMPLATE.
IT'S TRUE THAT SOME OF THE MORE *BESTIAL* FORMS ARE DIFFICULT TO CONTROL, BUT THE MAN WAS OF NO CONSEQUENCE.
HE HAD NO BACKGROUND, NO NAME. AN INCIDENTAL CHARACTER.

THERE ARE MORE IMPORTANT MATTERS TO BE CONSIDERED. THE IMPENDING *ANNIHILATION* OF THIS ENTIRE STRATUM, FOR INSTANCE.
ANIMAL MAN, PLEASE FOLLOW ME.
AH... I THINK HE *MEANS* IT.
QUICKLY!
LISTEN, I'D BETTER...
STOP!
STOP.
ALL OF YOU.
THIS CRAFT IS *MINE*. ITS SECRETS, ITS TREASURES: ALL MINE.
I UNCOVERED IT. IT IS *MINE*.
I'LL HOLD THEM.
WAIT...YOU CAN'T DO THAT ON YOUR OWN...
ANIMAL MAN, PLEASE...

DESTROY HER.
ARRRR!
I WILL DEAL WITH THE OTHERS.
OOOOOHHH
SHLLUKK!

...JESUS... OH, GOD... OHH...
...OHH...
OH.
IT'S... HEALED...
YAAAAA
EEEEURR
SHLAAAK!
OHHH.
...BITCH... I'LL KILL YOU... I'LL...

IS VIXEN GOING TO BE OKAY BACK THERE?
THE GREAT LIGHT YOU SEE IS A MANIFESTATION OF THE VAST ABSENCE THAT LIES BEHIND WHAT YOU CALL "REALITY."
FROM THAT LIGHT UNFOLDS THE CONTINUOUS PROCESS OF CREATION AND DESTRUCTION.
YOUR COMPANION WILL FIND THAT SHE CANNOT BE DESTROYED.
UNLESS, OF COURSE, WE FAIL IN OUR TASK.
WE'VE MET BEFORE, HAVEN'T WE? WHEN I'D JUST STARTED OUT AS ANIMAL MAN.
WEREN'T YOU TRYING TO INVADE EARTH OR SOMETHING?
A STANDARD DECEPTION. THIS SHIP, THE TRAVELLER, HAS BEEN BURIED HERE TEN THOUSAND YEARS. PERIODICALLY, WE ASSUME MEMORYFORMS AND TRAVEL TO THE SURFACE.
IN THE FORM OF ANANSE, THE SPIDER GOD, WE BROUGHT THE TANTU TOTEM TO MANKIND.
TWO THOUSAND YEARS LATER, IT WAS THE HELMET AND ELIXIR OF THE BEAST. THEN, THE SPIRIT MASKS. ALL THESE GIFTS PUT YOUR PEOPLE IN TOUCH WITH THE TEMPLATE.
FINALLY, WE ATTENDED YOUR CREATION. DO YOU REMEMBER THAT DAY?
YEAH, BUT...
YOU DID NOT SURVIVE THAT EXPLOSION. WE PLACED YOUR SPIRIT IN THE TEMPLATE AND GRAFTED ONTO YOUR ESSENCE THE ESSENCES OF THE BEAST AVATARS ALREADY THERE.
THEN WE REBUILT YOUR BODY, CELL BY CELL.
YOU WHAT?
YOUR "ANIMAL POWERS" DERIVE FROM THESE MORPHOGENETIC GRAFTS. THE GRAFTS WERE DAMAGED BY RECENT EVENTS AND WE HAVE BEEN FORCED TO DESTROY AND REBUILD YOU ONCE AGAIN.

THIS IS TOO WEIRD! I DON'T UNDERSTAND WHAT YOU'RE TELLING ME...
YOU WILL UNDERSTAND SOON. TERRIBLE TIMES ARE COMING BUT EVERYTHING WILL BECOME CLEAR.
NOW, YOU RECALL A CATASTROPHIC EVENT--THE "CRISIS"--THAT RECENTLY TOOK PLACE ON THIS STRATUM?
"THIS CRISIS, WE DISCOVERED, HAS RESULTED IN THE CURRENT THREAT TO YOUR REALITY.
"THE CONTINUUM WAS RADICALLY ALTERED AT THAT TIME BUT SOME HOLES REMAINED, UNSEEN, POCKETS OF CONTRADICTION."
YOUR LIFE WAS ONE SUCH CONTRADICTION. THE "ANIMAL MAN" WE CREATED WAS AN OLDER MAN IN A SIMPLER WORLD. HE SHOULD NOT HAVE EXISTED IN THE POST-CRISIS CONTINUUM, AND YET SOMEHOW YOUR HISTORY REMAINED UNALTERED.
YOU WERE LIVING IN A PARADOX. NOW THAT PARADOX THREATENS TO DESTROY THE STRUCTURE OF YOUR REALITY.
PUT YOUR HANDS IN HERE.
"YOU WERE REPAIRED FIRST, DO YOU UNDERSTAND? WE REBUILT YOUR MEMORIES WHILE YOUR ESSENCE WAS IN THE TEMPLATE.
"THAT MEANS THOSE MEMORIES CAN BE USED TO HEAL THE CONTINUUM."

DIRECT YOUR THOUGHTS INTO THE BREACH.
THE FORCES THAT ARE BEING RELEASED NOW WILL BE FELT ACROSS THE ENTIRE STRATUM, BUT IT'S STILL NOT TOO LATE TO PREVENT THE FINAL CATASTROPHIC UNBINDING.
IT'S FINISHED, OKAY?
THIS IS INSANE... IT CAN'T GO ON.
IF YOU FAIL, EVERYTHING IS LOST! YOUR FAMILY, YOUR FRIENDS, THE WORLD YOU KNEW!
REMEMBER!
IT'S FINISHED.
REMEMBER HOW IT WAS WHEN YOU FIRST BECAME ANIMAL MAN. BIND REALITY'S FABRIC WITH THOSE MEMORIES.
...HEAD HURTS... CONFUSED...
REMEMBER!
NO MORE.
NO MORE.

TEN YEARS AGO:

"I GUESS I MUST HAVE GOT THE POWERS WHEN THAT SPACESHIP OR WHATEVER IT WAS BLEW UP IN MY FACE.

"I DUNNO... MAYBE IT WAS *RADIATION* OR SOMETHING. AND THEN THERE WAS THAT THING...

"NO KIDDING, DUDE! IT'S OUT BACK IN THE WOODS. LIKE, IT TOTALLY FREAKED ME OUT!..."

WUHH?
IT'S OVER.
YOU SUCCEEDED.

IT'S ALL OVER, YOU...
NO!

IT'S NOT OVER FOR ME.
ONLY FOR YOU!

KRAK

NO!
WE ARE AGENTS OF THE POWER THAT BRINGS YOUR WORLD INTO BEING.

HOW CAN YOU HOPE TO HAVE POWER OVER US?

I HAVE SEEN CENTURIES PASS LIKE YEARS! I WILL NOT BE STOPPED BY YOU!

YOU HEAR ME? I'M HAMED ALI!
I AM HE WHO NEVER DIES!
YOU *HEAR* ME!?
YOU ARE *NOTHING*.

A MINOR CHARACTER. OLD-FASHIONED AND MELODRAMATIC. BEST FORGOTTEN.
YOUR STORY ENDS HERE.

NO! WAIT!
I AM HAMED ALI!

YOU DON'T UNDERSTAND... I CANNOT BE KILLED... I...

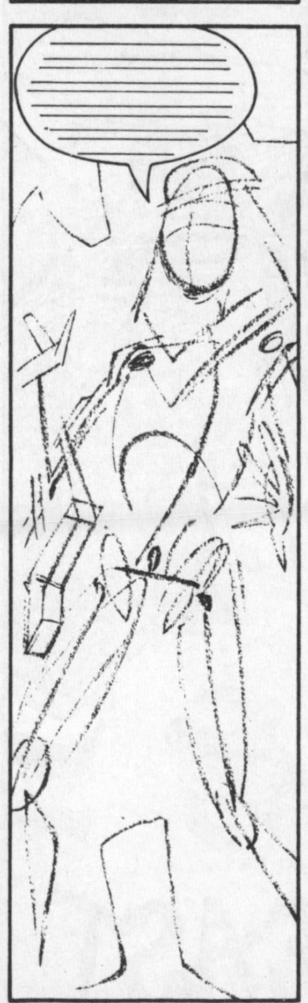

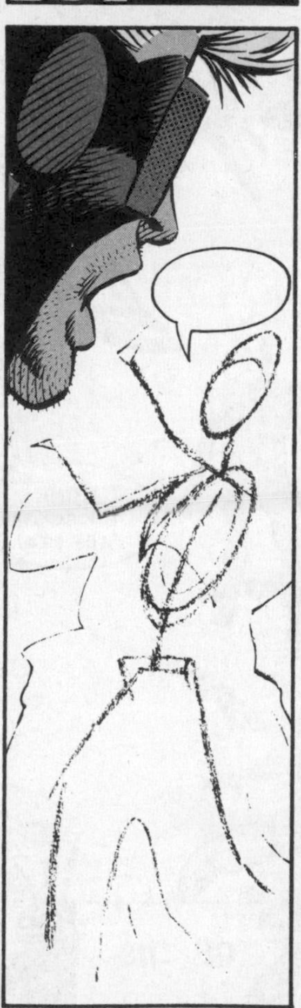

IT IS DONE.
WE MUST RELOCATE AND HEAL THE TRAVELLER. WE WILL MEET AGAIN, ANIMAL MAN.

WAIT! YOU HAVE TO *EXPLAIN* ALL THIS TO ME!
REMEMBER: TERRIBLE TIMES ARE COMING.
BE STRONG.
BE CAREFUL.

BEWARE.

I THINK THE GOOD GUYS WON.

NEXT: HOUR of the BEAST

DC
NEW FORMAT
13
JUL 89
US $1.50
CAN $1.85
UK 80p
Animal Man™
Morrison,
Truog &
Hazlewood

...SOUTH AFRICA-- AND ANOTHER OUTBREAK OF VIOLENCE IN THE BLACK TOWNSHIPS NEAR CAPE TOWN.
THIS REPORT FROM DON FRIEDMAN.

...LOOKS QUIET NOW BUT RUMORS OF A SERIOUS CLASH BETWEEN POLICE AND BLACK ACTIVISTS CONTINUE TO CIRCULATE.
GOVERNMENT FORCES CLAIM THAT THERE WERE "MINOR DISTURBANCES" BUT THAT, DESPITE A NUMBER OF ARRESTS, NO ONE WAS HURT.

BLACK CHURCH LEADERS, INCLUDING THE OUTSPOKEN ARCHBISHOP MOGATUSI... HAVE EXPRESSED CONCERN OVER RECENT OUTBREAKS OF VIOLENCE...
...AND THERE IS DEEP ANXIETY THAT A FURTHER PROTEST, AGAINST YESTERDAY'S DISTURBANCES, COULD LEAD TO NEW BLOODSHED.

THE SITUATION IN THIS COUNTRY IS RAPIDLY DETERIORATING. ANYONE CAN SEE THAT.
ARCHBISHOP MOGATUSI
IF THINGS ARE ALLOWED TO CONTINUE UNCHANGED, I FORESEE SERIOUS, VERY SERIOUS ERUPTIONS...

... DON FRIEDMAN. GBS NEWS.

CAPE TOWN.

THAT REPORT WAS COMPILED UNDER SOUTH AFRICAN GOVERNMENT RESTRICTIONS...

HOUR of the BEAST
GRANT MORRISON ○ writer
CHAS TRUOG &
DOUG HAZLEWOOD ○ artists
JOHN COSTANZA ○ letterer
TATJANA WOOD ○ colorist
ART YOUNG ○ asst. editor
KAREN BERGER ○ editor

...THIS IS SO WEIRD. I JUST SAW VIXEN ONTO THE PLANE AND THEN I RUN INTO YOU.
I GUESS I SHOULD BE GETTING USED TO WEIRDNESS BY NOW.

I MEAN, AFTER THE LAST FEW DAYS...
ANYWAY... LISTEN, I DON'T EVEN KNOW YOUR NAME.
cappuccino

AND I FEEL KINDA STUPID CALLING YOU B'WANA BEAST.
MAXWELL. MIKE MAXWELL.
DO I STILL HAVE TO CALL YOU ANIMAL MAN?

IT MUST BE NEARLY A YEAR NOW SINCE THE TWO OF US KNOCKED HELL OUT OF EACH OTHER IN THE SAN DIEGO ZOO, HUH?
THINGS SEEM TO BE GOING PRETTY WELL FOR YOU. I KEEP SEEING YOUR NAME IN MAGAZINES AND NEWSPAPERS...

YEAH... I SUPPOSE THINGS ARE WORKING OUT, BUT IT'S NOT REALLY LIKE WHAT I EXPECTED. I FEEL PRETTY MUCH THE SAME, YOU KNOW? I STILL GET DEPRESSED, I STILL ARGUE WITH MY WIFE ABOUT LEAVING THE TOILET SEAT UPRIGHT AND STUPID STUFF LIKE THAT.

THAT FIGHT WITH YOU, THOUGH-- IT CHANGED MY LIFE. REALLY.

I SUDDENLY REALIZED ALL THE TERRIBLE STUFF THAT WAS BEING DONE TO *ANIMALS*.

IT *WAS* A PRETTY WILD DAY.

"*REMEMBER?*

"IT'S FUNNY; SOME SAY THAT THE SUPERHEROES ARE THE NEXT STAGE IN HUMAN EVOLUTION, YET EVERY TIME WE MEET, ALL WE SEEM TO DO IS FIGHT ONE ANOTHER. IF THAT'S THE FUTURE, IT DOESN'T LOOK TOO BRIGHT TO ME."

SO. WHAT KIND OF YEAR HAVE *YOU* HAD?

TRAVELING MOSTLY. IT TOOK ME A *LONG* TIME TO GET OVER WHAT HAPPENED LAST YEAR AND TO *PREPARE* MYSELF FOR WHAT I HAVE TO DO NOW.

SEE, I JUST CAN'T CONTINUE AS B'WANA BEAST. IT'S BECOME... WELL, IT'S BECOME *IMPOSSIBLE*.

ANYWAY, I'M REQUIRED TO FULFILL ONE LAST FUNCTION.

I HAVE TO FIND THE *NEW* BEAST, MY *SUCCESSOR*.

YOU WANT TO COME ALONG? I MAY BE ABLE TO USE SOME HELP.
WELL... I...
AH, WHY NOT?
I WANTED TO SEE SOME OF THE *REAL* AFRICA ANYWAY.
WHERE ARE WE HEADED?
SOUTH INTO *TANZANIA*.
TO THE *HOME* OF THE BEAST.
"TO KILIMANJARO."

...AS FAR AS I CAN MAKE OUT, I WAS ONLY THE *SECOND* WHITE MAN TO BE CHOSEN TO SERVE AS THE BEAST.
THERE WAS ANOTHER GUY, A HUNDRED YEARS AGO. A BRITISH *SOLDIER*, A DESERTER FROM THE *BOER WAR*.
THOSE *ALIENS* I TOLD YOU ABOUT CLAIMED THAT *THEY* CREATED THE HELMET AND THE ELIXIR.
I STILL FEEL LIKE I *DREAMED* THAT WHOLE THING.
ALL *I* KNOW IS THAT THE LEGEND OF THE *BEAST* GOES WAY BACK. IT TURNS UP IN THE STORY OF *MKUNARE* AND *KANYANGA*, ONE OF THE OLDEST FOLK MYTHS IN EAST AFRICA.
MY PART IN THE *MYTHOLOGY'S* ALMOST OVER NOW, I GUESS. SOMETIMES I WISH I'D *TRIED* A LITTLE HARDER...
AH, FORGET IT.
NEVER COULD GET USED TO THE TASTE OF THIS STUFF.
AA

THERE! CAN YOU HEAR THEM!?
FOOTSTEPS! GROWING LOUDER!
A MILLION FOOTFALLS!
LISTEN! IN THE DEEP WALLS OF KILIMANJARO! THE NETHERSTONE OF THE WORLD FROM WHICH TIME IS GROUND! THE AXLE ABOUT WHICH THE EARTH TURNS!
LISTEN! THE FOOTSTEPS OF A CONTINENT!
WHICH ONE? WHICH IN ALL THIS NOISE?
STEPS FALL AWAY. FALL AWAY.
ONLY ONE. ONLY ONE WALKS THIS WAY. ONLY ONE.
WHERE WHERE WHERE? WHICH WILL IT BE?
I
I
YES.

... ARE YOU TRYING TO COMMIT SUICIDE, DOMINIC? I HEARD YOU WALKING THE WHOLE LENGTH OF THAT RAMP...
THIS IS INSANE!
WHITES ONLY
YOU'RE IN THE WHITE DISTRICT AFTER CURFEW. IF YOU GET CAUGHT, IT'S IMMEDIATE DETENTION WITHOUT TRIAL AND...
WHITES ONLY
YOU THINK I DON'T KNOW THESE THINGS, DAVID?
I HAD TO MEET YOU TONIGHT. IT'S MY LAST CHANCE BEFORE YOU LEAVE FOR LONDON.
WE MUST GET THESE PICTURES OUT OF THE COUNTRY. YOU'RE OUR ONLY CHANCE TO SHOW PEOPLE WHAT'S HAPPENING HERE.
I KNOW. I KNOW. BUT AN UNDEVELOPED SPOOL, DOMINIC...
I HAD NO FACILITIES. IT'S ALL OR NOTHING, DAVID. YOU CAN HIDE THE SPOOL IN YOUR OWN CAMERA, EH?
YEAH. GOD ALMIGHTY! WHY AM I DOING THIS?
YOU'RE DOING IT BECAUSE IT FEELS GOOD TO DO RIGHT SOMETIMES.
DON'T LET ME DOWN, DAVID.

CHUDD

NICE NIGHT FOR A STROLL, KAFFIR.
WUFF

UHHH NO
NO

ARE YOU SURE IT DOESN'T HURT THE ANIMALS WHEN YOU USE YOUR FUSION POWER ON THEM?
THE ANIMALS DON'T CARE ONE WAY OR THE OTHER. WHEN THEIR JOB IS DONE, THEY'LL RETURN HERE AND TAKE UP THEIR LIVES WHERE THEY LEFT OFF.
ANIMALS DON'T THINK AS WE DO. HUMAN SENTIMENTALITY HAS NO PLACE IN THEIR EXISTENCE.
THERE.
IT MAY BE DANGEROUS TO ENTER SOUTH AFRICAN AIRSPACE, ANIMAL MAN.
STAY LOW AND DON'T FORGET RADAR.
NOW.
LET'S TRACK DOWN THE BEAST.

CLA-CHAKK LAK
WELL, WELL, WELL. DOMINIC MNDAWE. WE'VE WAITED FAR TOO LONG TO GET YOU DOWN HERE, KAFFIR.
AND DON'T WORRY ABOUT THE PHOTOGRAPHS. WE'LL PICK MR. QUINN UP AT THE AIRPORT ON THURSDAY.
YOU'RE BECOMING A DANGEROUS MAN, YOU KNOW THAT?
DANGEROUS MEN MEET WITH BAD ENDS. SAY "YES, MR. VAN de VOORT."
...YES... MR. VAN de VOORT...
THAT'S RIGHT. THEY DIE ON HUNGER STRIKE. THEY FALL OUT OF WINDOWS OR DOWN STAIRS. ACCIDENTALLY, OF COURSE. THEY HANG THEMSELVES.
NOBODY CARES.

THIS CELL STINKS. YOU'RE SUPPOSED TO USE THE BUCKET.
OR IS THAT TOO SOPHISTICATED FOR THE LIKES OF YOU?
OH YES, YOU'RE A DANGEROUS MAN, BUT YOU'RE STILL ONLY SMALL FRY.
YOU'RE STILL ONLY AN ILL-EDUCATED SAVAGE WITH A CHIP ON HIS SHOULDER.
AND YOU... ARE A WELL-EDUCATED ONE, I SUPPOSE?
WHOKK!
THE MAN WE WANT IS ARCHBISHOP MOGATUSI.
BUT HOW DO YOU PIN DOWN A MAN LIKE THAT? HOW DO YOU GET HIM RIGHT WHERE YOU WANT HIM?
PERHAPS YOU ARRANGE A LITTLE "DISTURBANCE". PERHAPS YOU WHIP THE NATIVES INTO A FRENZY. PERHAPS THE ARCHBISHOP IS MANEUVERED INTO A POSITION WHERE HE FINDS HIMSELF CALLED UPON TO CALM HIS PEOPLE IN ORDER TO AVOID FURTHER BLOOD-SHED.
AND PERHAPS HE IS ARRESTED FOR ADDRESSING AN ILLEGAL GATHERING, EH?

ONE OF MY FAVORITE STORIES, WHEN I WAS VERY YOUNG, WAS THE STORY OF THE UNICORN. EVERY NIGHT, I WOULD BEG MY MOTHER, "TELL ME ABOUT THE UNICORN!"

"IT WAS A FIERCE, UNTAMEABLE BEAST, THE UNICORN. OH, IT LOOKED BEAUTIFUL AND INNOCENT BUT THAT TERRIBLE HORN WAS MADE FOR KILLING.
"THE ONLY THING THAT COULD PLACATE THE UNICORN WAS A VIRGIN. A SPOTLESS MAID."

THE BEAST WOULD LAY ITS HEAD IN HER LAP, SURRENDER ITSELF TO HER PROTECTION...

"AND THEN, WHEN THE UNICORN WAS DEFENSELESS, THE HUNTERS WOULD STRIKE.
"VERY FREUDIAN, EH?"

WE DECIDED NOT TO USE A VIRGIN TO LURE THE ARCHBISHOP, BUT THE PRINCIPLE IS THE SAME. WE'LL HAVE HIM TOMORROW.
YOUR DREAM OF BLACK SUPREMACY IN SOUTH AFRICA IS LIKE THE UNICORN; IT EXISTS ONLY IN A SICK FANTASY.

NOW.
WHY DON'T YOU PUT YOUR NECK THROUGH HERE AND SPARE YOURSELF A GREAT DEAL OF PAIN?

COME ON.
ON YOUR FEET, KAFFIR.
CAN'T... MY LEG IS BROKEN...
ON YOUR BLOODY FEET OR I'LL BREAK MORE THAN YOUR...
KREEEEEE
RAAKKSH
WHAT IN THE NAME OF
WHOK
THIS IS HIM?
YEAH.
THE NEW BEAST.

AND I'M WARNING YOU NOW-- THE BEAST BELONGS TO MYTHOLOGY. IT WAS HERE BEFORE THE WHITES AND IT WILL STILL BE HERE WHEN THEY'VE GONE. IT'S BEYOND POLITICS.

IN SOUTH AFRICA, MR. MAXWELL, NOTHING IS "BEYOND POLITICS" ANYMORE.

LET ME TELL YOU SOMETHING.

WHEN I WAS TEN YEARS OLD, I WAS ONE OF THE CHILDREN WHO WENT ON STRIKE IN SOWETO.
WE WERE REFUSING TO LEARN AFRIKAANS IN OUR SCHOOLS. REFUSING TO LEARN THE LANGUAGE OF OPPRESSION.

"I'LL BE HONEST, FOR ME THERE WAS NO IDEOLOGY INVOLVED THEN. IT WAS TIME AWAY FROM SCHOOL, THAT'S ALL.
FREEDOM
"AND THEN THEY SENT IN THE TROOPS.

"I WAS HALF-BLINDED BY TEAR GAS AND BADLY WOUNDED IN THE THIGH, BUT AT LEAST I SURVIVED.
"MORE THAN SEVEN HUNDRED CHILDREN WERE KILLED THAT DAY. THOUSANDS WERE INJURED."

WHERE WAS B'WANA BEAST THEN, MR. MAXWELL?
WHERE WAS THE AFRICAN HERO WHEN AFRICAN CHILDREN WERE DYING?
I TELL YOU, IT WON'T HAPPEN AGAIN.

IT'S NOT ABOUT POLITICS.

GUESS YOU TOUCHED A NERVE THERE.
ABOUT TOMORROW-- COUNT ME IN, OKAY?
THERE'S SOMETHING I'D LIKE YOU TO DO BEFORE THEN, ANIMAL MAN. IT CONCERNS A MAN NAMED DAVID QUINN.
RIGHT NOW, HOWEVER, I THINK WE SHOULD DRINK A TOAST.

TODAY'S POLITICS IS TOMORROW'S MYTHOLOGY.

STAY RIGHT WHERE YOU ARE!
NOT ONE MORE STEP!

LET ME WARN YOU! THIS CONSTITUTES AN ILLEGAL GATHERING!
YOU HAVE THREE MINUTES TO DISPERSE AND RETURN TO YOUR HOMES!

I REPEAT, THREE...
CRZZZKK! BROTHERS AND SISTERS! PLEASE RETURN TO YOUR HOMES PEACEFULLY!
THIS IS NOT THE WAY! DON'T GIVE THEM ANY MORE EXCUSES. YOU ARE BEING LED INTO A TRAP!
PLEASE RETURN TO YOUR HOMES!

IT'S MOGATUSI! THE SLY OLD BASTARD'S BROAD-CASTING!
HE MUST BE SOMEWHERE NEAR.

VIOLENCE IS NOT THE ANSWER, BROTHERS AND SISTERS! IT IS THE WAY OF OUR OPPRESSORS!
I BEG YOU TO RETURN TO YOUR HOMES!

I DON'T WANT THIS CROWD DISPERSED.
YOU 'RE IN CHARGE, SERGEANT.
SIR.

DON'T LET THESE ANIMALS WALK AWAY.
ON MY ORDER...
STOP!

FIRE ON THESE PEOPLE AND YOU FIRE ON ME.
IT WON'T BE SO EASY TO EXPLAIN THE DEATH OF AN AMERICAN.

YOU HEAR ME. THIS HAS GONE FAR ENOUGH!
IT'S FINISHED!

YOU'RE PATHETIC.
CHOOM
FIRE AT...
RRRRRRRRMMMMMM

MMMMMMBBBBLLL
MY GOD!
MY GOD, WHAT'S...

LLLLRRRRMMMB

CRRRK

CHUNT
PLUTCH

SO.
HOW DID I DO?
FRRRUNCH

MOGATUSI!
THRAATCH

RIGHT!
YOU'RE BLOODY *FINISHED*, YOU...

VAN de VOORT!

WHAT'S...
oh god
oh my god

...WELL, THE WHOLE THING TURNED INTO KIND OF A ROUT, BUT AT LEAST WE STOPPED IT FROM BEING A MASSACRE.
HOW'S THE ARM?

HURTS LIKE HELL BUT IT WAS WORTH IT TO SEE THOSE BASTARDS RUNNING SCARED.
FOR A WHILE THERE I WAS SURE I'D BURROWED UNDER THE WRONG...
HEY, LOOK.

DOMINIC.
THE BEAST. NOT B'WANA BEAST NOW, BUT FREEDOM BEAST.
THERE WILL BE REPRISALS FOR WHAT WE DID TODAY.

YEAH. THAT'S WHY I'M STAYING ON HERE.
YOU HAVE A FEW LESSONS TO LEARN, DOMINIC.
THE ARCHBISHOP GOT AWAY?
HE'S SAFE.

AND THE OTHER GUY? VAN de VOORT?
HE DIED.
HE DIED OF A RARE DISEASE.

SYMBOLISM.

EPILOGUE:
...I HARDLY NEED TO SAY THAT THE WHOLE THING'S BEEN SOMETHING OF AN EMBARRASSMENT TO THE SECURITY SERVICES, MINISTER.
AND *THESE* ARE THE PHOTOGRAPHS *QUINN* WAS CARRYING? THESE ARE WHY HE WAS STOPPED AT THE AIRPORT?

DAILY PL

MY GOD.
HOLIDAY SNAPS.

WHERE CAN I FIND YOUR *EDITOR*?
MR. *WHITE*? AH... THAT DOOR BACK THERE.

HOLIDAY SNAPS!

PERRY WHITE
EDITOR
MR. WHITE?
GOT SOMETHING FOR YOU.

NEXT: SPOOKS

DC
NEW FORMAT
14
AUG 89
US $1.50
CAN $1.85
UK 80p
Animal Man™
DADDY...

HELLO.

HELLO, MAXINE.
SPOOKS
GRANT MORRISON ○ writer
TOM GRUMMETT &
STEVE MONTANO ○ artists
JOHN COSTANZA ○ letterer
TATJANA WOOD ○ colorist
ART YOUNG ○ asst. editor
KAREN BERGER ○ editor
ABCDE

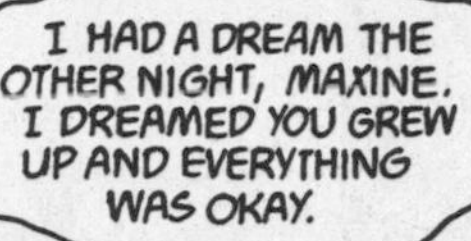
I HAD A DREAM THE OTHER NIGHT, MAXINE. I DREAMED YOU GREW UP AND EVERYTHING WAS OKAY.

YOU CAN'T EVEN *HEAR* ME, CAN YOU? I CAN'T EVEN *WARN* YOU.
OH, MAXINE.

...MAXINE...

I MISS YOU.
I MISS YOU ALL SO MUCH.

MAXINE!
MAXINE!

...MAXINE...?

WHO WAS THAT *MAN* YOU WERE TALKING TO?
I *TOLD* YOU! NEVER, *EVER* SPEAK TO STRANGE MEN...

IT *WASN'T* A STRANGE MAN.
IT WAS *DADDY*.

WHY WAS HE *CRYING*, MOMMY?

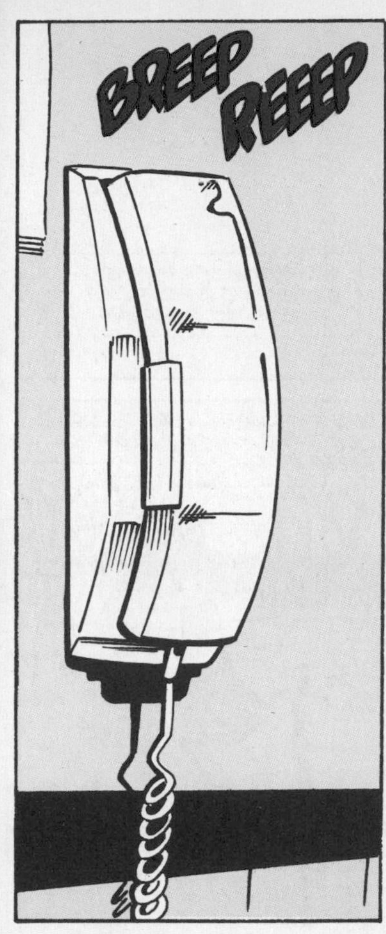
BREEP REEEP

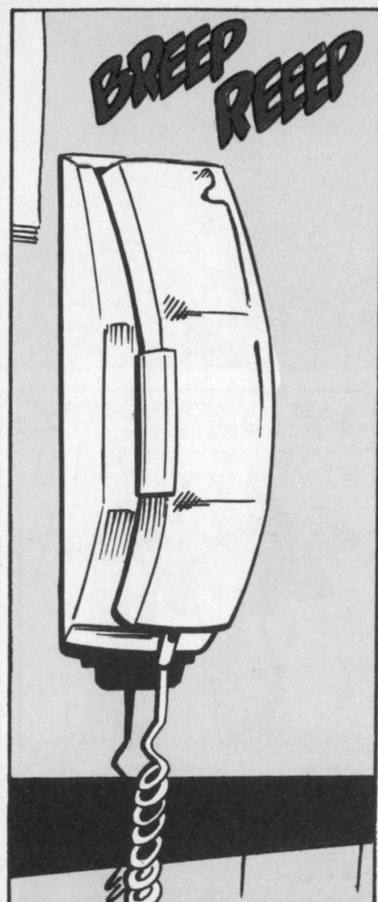
BREEP REEEP

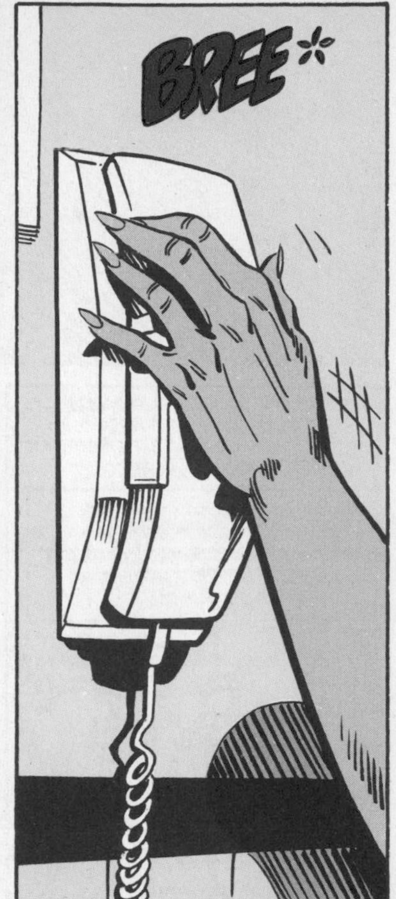
BREE*

UH-HUH?
BUDDY! LISTEN, WHAT ARE YOU DOING? WERE YOU OUT BACK A...
YOU'RE WHERE?

THE AIRPORT?
OH. RIGHT.

RAIN ON THE CANAL.
INTERFERENCE PATTERNS OF CONCENTRIC CIRCLES LIKE BOMB IMPACT DIAGRAMS.

LIKE TELEPATHIC POWERS IN COMICS. LIKE THE CUP AND RING MARKS ON MEGALITHIC STONES. LIKE PATTERNS ON A HOLOGRAPHIC PLATE.

THE SYMBOL OF DAVID BOHM'S IMPLICATE ORDER THEORY. A VISION OF A VAST, INTERCONNECTED UNIVERSE WHERE EVERY PART CONTAINS THE WHOLE.

WHERE THE UNIVERSE IS A MIRROR REFLECTING ITSELF.
EVERYTHING IS EVERYTHING.

DUCKS SQUABBLE IN THE REEDS. RAIN BLOWS ALONG THE TOWPATH. I NEED AN IDEA.
"THE WIND DOTH BLOW TO-DAY MY LOVE, AND A FEW SMALL DROPS OF RAIN; I NEVER HAD BUT ONE TRUE LOVE;

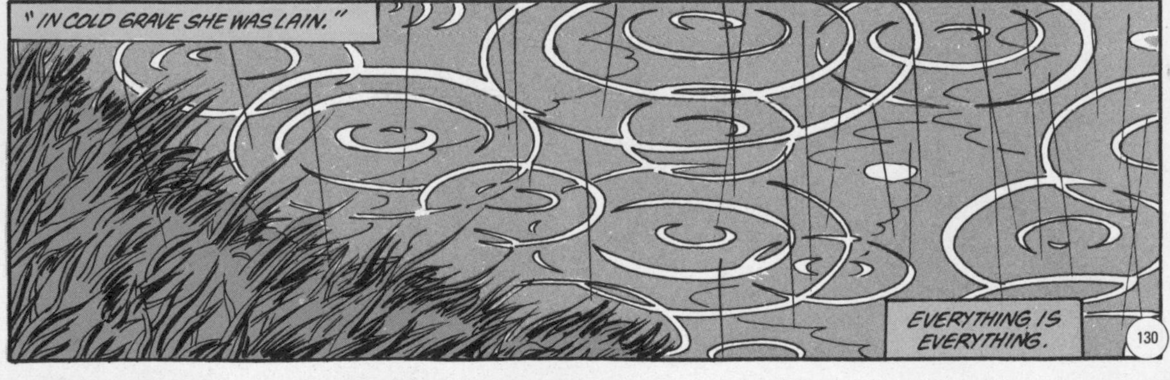
"IN COLD GRAVE SHE WAS LAIN."
EVERYTHING IS EVERYTHING.

"THE UNQUIET GRAVE." I USED TO LOVE THAT WHEN I WAS AT SCHOOL.
CHRIST. EASY PLEASED.
GASWORKS AGAINST A RESTLESS SKY, THE BONES OF MACHINE-AGE DINOSAURS. HIDEOUS METAPHOR.
WHAT'LL IT BE NEXT?
CHOICE EXTRACTS FROM THE OXFORD DICTIONARY OF QUOTATIONS? TROTTING OUT THE NIETZSCHE AND THE SHELLEY AND THE SHAKESPEARE TO DIGNIFY SOME OLD COSTUMED CLAPTRAP?
PROBABLY.
SOMETIMES YOU WONDER, IN AN INTERCONNECTED UNIVERSE, WHO'S DREAMING WHO?
LOCK 27
HIGHWATER.
WAKE UP.
WAKE UP.

WUHH!

...WALLS. LEMON LIGHT. HOTEL SHEETS. THIS BOX OF STILL AIR.
ELECTRIC CLOCK BUZZING.

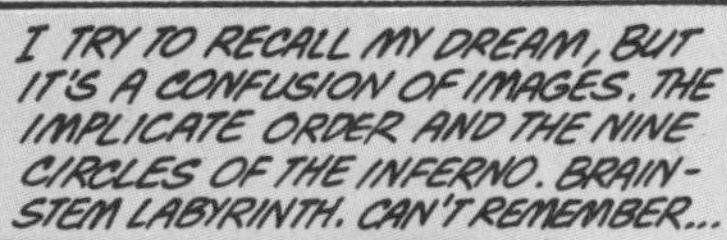
I TRY TO RECALL MY DREAM, BUT IT'S A CONFUSION OF IMAGES. THE IMPLICATE ORDER AND THE NINE CIRCLES OF THE INFERNO. BRAIN-STEM LABYRINTH. CAN'T REMEMBER...

"WORDS ARE UGLY WHEN THEY TRAVEL IN PACKS."

HAH! WHERE DID THAT COME FROM?
I SHOULD WRITE IT DOWN.

THAT'S WHAT I GET FOR EATING CHILI AT THREE-THIRTY IN THE MORNING.
NOW...

WHERE THE HELL AM I?

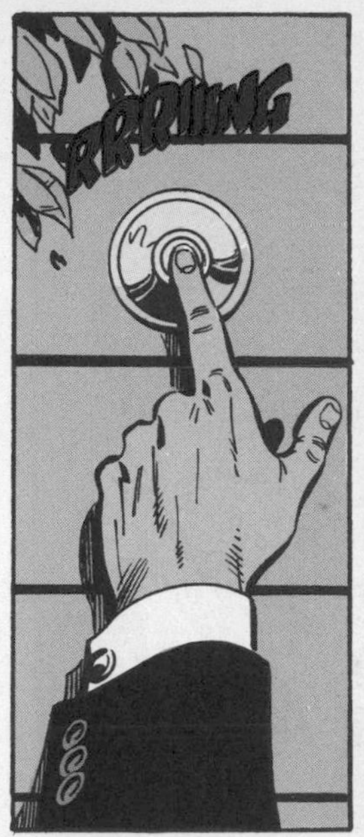
RRRIIING

YES?

AH! MRS. LINFIELD, I PRESUME?
MY NAME'S LENNOX. I HOPE YOU DON'T MIND ME CALLING, BUT I WONDERED IF YOU MIGHT SPARE A FEW MOMENTS TO HEAR THE GOOD NEWS.

WHAT?...
THAT'S RIGHT. THE WONDERFUL NEWS OF GOD'S KINGDOM ON EARTH. PERHAPS YOU MIGHT BE INTERESTED IN SOME OF OUR LITERATURE.
the Lookout
ARE YOU READY FOR GOD'S KINGDOM'?
AWAKE

OH, I SEE.
WELL, TO BE PERFECTLY HONEST, MR...AH...MR. LENNOX, I'M NOT A PARTICULARLY RELIGIOUS PERSON AT ALL, AND IT WOULDN'T REALLY BE FAIR TO WASTE YOUR...
MOM!

MOM, IF TERESA CALLS, WILL YOU TELL HER I'M ON MY...

MOM?...
MOM, HE'S GOT A...

NG
the LOOKOU
ARE Y
READY FOR
GOD'S
KINGDOM?

...WELL, WHAT DOES IT LOOK LIKE?
IT'S A WEE-JA BOARD, DUMMY!
ABCDEFGHIJKLM
NOPQRSTUVWXYZ
1234567890
GOOD BYE
YES
Ouija

I FOUND IT IN SOME OLD SUIT-CASE ALONG WITH A WHOLE PILE OF PENTHOUSE AND STUFF.
USED TO BELONG TO MY BROTHER, THE CREEP!
I DON'T KNOW ABOUT THIS...

I CAN'T BELIEVE YOU! YOUR DAD'S, LIKE, A SUPERHERO AND YOU'RE SCARED OF JUST ABOUT EVERYTHING, MAN!
I DIDN'T SAY I WAS SCARED...

YOU DIDN'T HAVE TO. I SAW THE STAIN ON YOUR PANTS.
SCREW YOU, SHELTON.
SO WHAT DO WE DO?

YOU GUYS PUT YOUR FINGERS ON THE PLANCHETTE, OKAY?
RIGHT.
OUIJA
Ouija
123456789
GOOD BYE

UM.
IS THERE ANYBODY THERE?

OH, WOW.
BREEP REEEP
AAAAA

HI.
YOU'RE *PUSHING* IT, ERIC!
I AM *NOT!*
LOOK.

LOOK!
YOU GETTING ALL THIS DOWN, GARY?

YEAH. *C.L.I.F.*
F AGAIN. IT'S *YOU,* CLIFF.

IT'S ME *WHAT?*
THE SPOOKS SAY, *"CLIFF BAKER IS A WALKING DORK,"* MAN...

Ouija
WHAT'S IT DOING NOW?

THERE.
ANYTHING ELSE?
CLIFF
9
22

IS... WHAT'S IT DOING...?
HOW COME IT'S *SHAKING*? WHAT'S IT MEAN WHEN IT SHAKES?...
HOW SHOULD *I* KNOW?

THIS IS *WAY* TOO WEIRD. REALLY.
DON'T TAKE YOUR FINGER OFF YET!
YOU'RE NOT SUPPOSED TO...

KLESSSH

RADICAL!
I'M *CUT*.
HEY, YOU GUYS, I'M CUT!

FIRST BLOOD TO THE SPOOKS.

CLIFF
9
27

UH-HUH... SURE. YEAH. I'LL GIVE HIM THE MESSAGE AS SOON AS HE GETS BACK...
YEAH... NICE TO HEAR FROM YOU TOO, *DANE.* I WILL, YEAH... OKAY. YOU TOO...
BYE.

CLIK

SEPTEMBER

SEPTEMBER

MAXINE!
HEY!
MAXINE, PICK UP YOUR STUFF AND...
ELLEN?
YAAAAAAA
ELLEN?
MY GOD, ELLEN. IT'S ME!
IT'S ONLY ME.

SAN FRANCISCO. I MUST HAVE COME HERE BECAUSE ANIMAL MAN WORKS FROM THE WEST COAST.
I'VE COME TO FIND ANIMAL MAN.
I'VE FOLLOWED A PAPERCHASE FROM COAST TO COAST, BUT IT'S ALMOST OVER. WHATEVER IT IS, IT'S ALMOST OVER.
"THE UNIVERSE IS A MIRROR..."
WAS THAT THE DREAM?
BEST NOT TO TOUCH IT.
I MIGHT FALL THROUGH.
PERHAPS I ALREADY HAVE.

THERE'S NOBODY HERE, ELLEN. REALLY.
I'VE CHECKED THE WHOLE PLACE.
IT'S PRETTY WILD OUT.
YOU KNOW, MORRIS WEIDEMEIR SAID SOMETHING FUNNY TODAY. YOU KNOW WHAT MORRIS IS LIKE--HE STOPS ME OUT IN THE STREET AND SAYS, "YOU'RE GETTING TOO FAMOUS TO TALK TO YOUR NEIGHBORS, HUH?"
HE SAYS HE CALLED TO ME ON MONDAY AND THAT I JUST IGNORED HIM.
I WAS IN AFRICA ON MONDAY.
THAT'S WHAT I'VE BEEN SAYING, BUDDY. THINGS HAVE BEEN REALLY WEIRD WHILE YOU'VE BEEN AWAY.
I MEAN, I SAW THIS GUY AND MAXINE SWEARS IT WAS YOU.
YEAH.
I STILL DON'T KNOW WHAT HAPPENED IN AFRICA. I WAS BEING TOLD SOMETHING BUT I COULDN'T GRASP IT. I WAS ON THE EDGE OF SOMETHING SO... I DON'T KNOW... SO AWESOME...

I HATE THIS WIND AND THIS DARK.
EVERYTHING SEEMS SO... VULNERABLE.
EVEN CLIFF WAS ACTING STRANGE WHEN HE WENT TO BED TONIGHT.
I MEAN, WHEN WAS THE LAST TIME HE USED THAT SUPERMAN NIGHTLIGHT? IT'S...
...BUDDY...
IT'S HIM!
IT'S HIM!

THERE'S NO ONE HERE.

LISTEN, JUST STAY HERE, ELLEN. STAY WITH THE KIDS, OKAY?

I WON'T BE LONG.

WHO'S THERE?

LISTEN, WHAT DO YOU WANT?
JUST TELL ME...
I KNOW YOU.
WHEN I WAS TEN. MY GOD. I SAW YOU.
I KNOW YOU.

WELL?...
NOTHING.
I DON'T KNOW.
SPOOKS.
NEXT: THE DEVIL and the DEEP BLUE SEA

DC
NEW FORMAT
15
SEP 89
US $1.50
CAN $1.85
UK 80p
Animal Man™
Morrison, Truog & Hazlewood

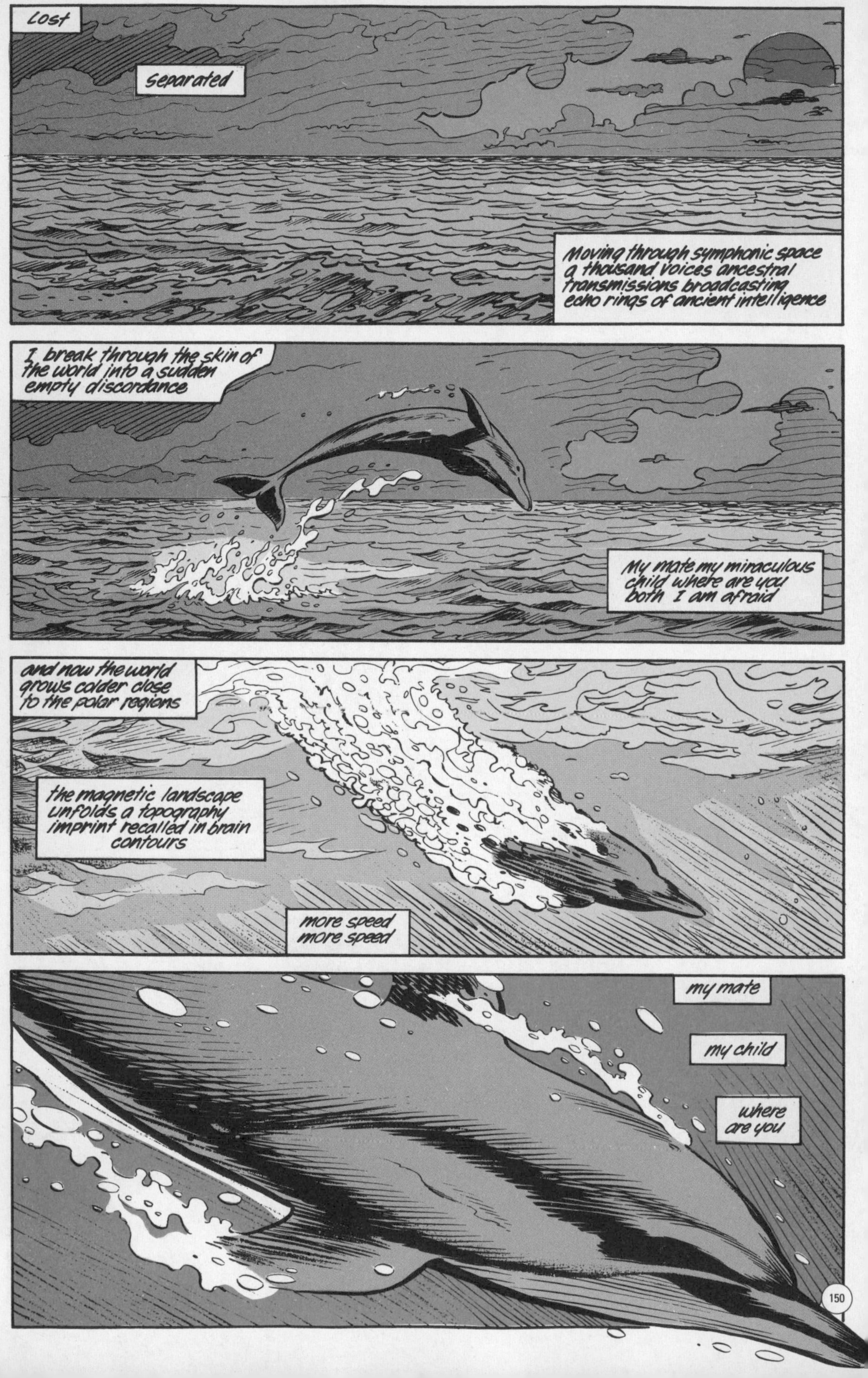

Lost

separated

Moving through symphonic space a thousand voices ancestral transmissions broadcasting echo rings of ancient intelligence

I break through the skin of the world into a sudden empty discordance

My mate my miraculous child where are you both I am afraid

...I STILL THINK COMING HERE WAS A BIG MISTAKE, DANE...

CALM DOWN, JÓANNES, WILL YOU? THE PLACE IS PACKED TONIGHT AFTER THE CANADIANS BROUGHT IN THAT SHIPMENT OF WHISKEY.
NO ONE'S INTERESTED IN US.
GUINNE

MAYBE. BUT I JUST CAUGHT SIGHT OF ONGUR NIELSEN AT THE BAR.
THAT GUY'S BAD NEWS, DANE.

YEAH, WELL, I'M BAD NEWS, TOO. THE WORST HE'S EVER HEARD.
DON'T WORRY, OKAY? WE'VE GOT DOLPHIN AND WHO KNOWS, BUDDY MIGHT STILL TURN UP.

IF HE HASN'T GOTTEN TOO BIG TO REMEMBER OLD FRIENDS, THAT IS.
BELIEVE ME, JÓANNES, EVERYTHING'S GOING TO BE JUST FINE.
SURE. SURE.

WE *KNOW* WHO YOU ARE, AMERICAN.

ANOTHER BLEEDING HEART *ENVIRONMENTALIST* WHO THINKS HE HAS THE RIGHT TO INTERFERE IN OUR CULTURE.

DANE DORRANCE, THE "*SEA DEVIL*."

CLUDD
WHUFF
WHOKK
ONGUR! FOR GOD'S SAKE, IT'S...
ONGUR... PLEASE... I DON'T WANT *TROUBLE*...
SHUT UP!
KOOM
OHHHH
WELL...

The Devil and the Deep Blue Sea
GRANT MORRISON writer
CHAS TRUOG and DOUG HAZLEWOOD artists
JOHN COSTANZA letterer
TATJANA WOOD colorist
ART YOUNG assoc. editor
KAREN BERGER editor
WAS IT SOMETHING I SAID?

WHAT EXACTLY DID YOU *DO* BACK THERE, BUDDY? MY HEAD'S STILL RINGING.

AH, IT WAS JUST A TRICK I PICKED UP FROM A *PISTOL SHRIMP.*

THEY'RE ABLE TO SNAP THEIR CLAWS TOGETHER TO PRODUCE SONIC BLASTS.

STUNS PREY.

IT LOOKED TO ME LIKE I GOT HERE JUST IN TIME.

IT'S KIND OF FUNNY TO GET TO MY AGE AND FIND THAT YOU'VE TURNED INTO A *TERRORIST,* BUT I GUESS THAT'S WHAT I AM--AN ECO-TERRORIST.
JÓANNES HERE IS ANOTHER ONE OF THE GOOD GUYS. I'D BE LOST IN THESE WATERS WITHOUT HIM.

ANIMAL MAN. IS GOOD TO SEE YOU.
HI THERE.

MANY OF US HERE ARE CONCERNED ABOUT WHAT IS GOING ON.
WE ARE ANXIOUS TO SHOW THAT NOT *ALL* THE PEOPLE OF *FAROYAR* ARE LIKE ONGUR.
SO WHAT CAN I DO TO HELP?

EVERY YEAR, THESE WATERS SEE A MASSIVE INFLUX OF *DOLPHINS,* HEADING NORTH, HUGE *SCHOOLS* OF THEM.
AND EVERY YEAR THE FAROESE *SLAUGHTER* THOSE DOLPHINS. FOR *FUN.*
WE'RE HERE TO *STOP* IT THIS YEAR.

WHEN I READ ABOUT WHAT YOU'VE BEEN DOING FOR *ANIMALS* BACK HOME, I FIGURED YOU MIGHT WANT IN ON THIS. *AND* THAT YOUR POWERS COULD PROVE INVALUABLE.
WE MISSED THE FIRST SCHOOL. IT WAS *TERRIBLE.*
I WON'T SEE THAT HAPPEN AGAIN.

YOU WANT TO GO SWIMMING?

"BOATS WERE USED TO HERD THAT FIRST SCHOOL TOWARDS THE SHORE.
"THE NOISE CONFUSES THEM, FRIGHTENS THEM. THEY'RE DRIVEN INTO THE SHALLOWS.
"AND THAT'S WHERE THE ISLANDERS ARE WAITING, WITH HOOKS AND ROPES AND FLENSING KNIVES.
"IT'S A BIG SPECTACLE; DRAWS PEOPLE FROM MILES AROUND. THEY COME IN CARS, BRING THE KIDS ALONG.
"IT'S JUST LIKE THE CIRCUS.
"IT GOES ON FOR A LONG TIME... SCREAMING... BLADES GRINDING AGAINST SPINES. PEOPLE CARVING THEIR NAMES INTO THE FACES OF TERRIFIED DOLPHINS, HACKING OFF THE FLUKES FOR SOUVENIRS...
"AND THE CHILDREN...
"THE MEN CUT FETUSES FROM THE BODIES OF PREGNANT DOLPHINS AND GIVE THEM TO THE CHILDREN TO PLAY WITH.
"TO PLAY WITH."

EVERY YEAR.
A LONG TIME AGO, THE FAROESE KILLED DOLPHINS OUT OF NECESSITY, FOR SURVIVAL. NOW IT'S JUST SPORT.

NOW IT'S SIMPLY SLAUGHTER, DISGUISED AS "TRADITION,"

AND IT'S NOT ONLY DOLPHINS.

"THE ANNUAL GRIND TAKES ITS TOLL OF ALREADY ENDANGERED WHALE SPECIES.
"JÓANNES TELLS ME HE'S SEEN THE SURF COME IN RED FOR DAYS AFTER A GRIND.

"WE'VE EVEN SEEN RUSSIAN FACTORY SHIPS OPERATING ILLEGALLY IN THESE WATERS, FLOUTING INTER-NATIONAL WHALING AGREEMENTS IN RETURN FOR CRATES OF VODKA.
"MANKIND IS SO STUPID, BUDDY. WHY CAN'T WE SEE BEYOND A QUICK BUCK? EVEN IF WE REFUSE TO SEE THAT CETACEANS ARE HIGHLY INTELLIGENT, IT'S...
"... I MEAN, WHALES EAT PLANKTON, RIGHT?

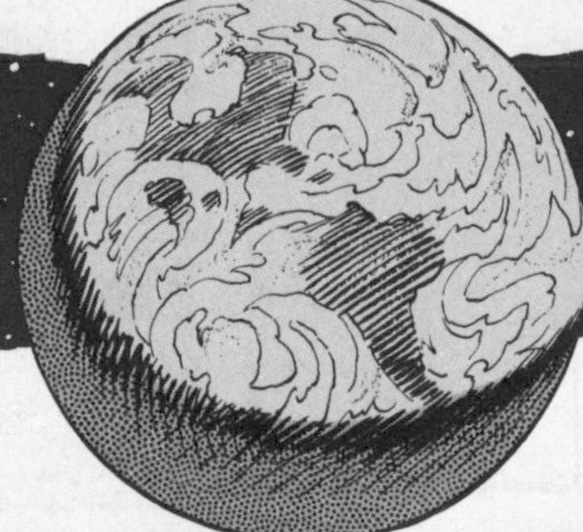
"DID YOU KNOW THAT 70% OF THE WORLD'S OXYGEN IS PRODUCED BY PLANKTON? WITHOUT THE WHALES TO CONTROL IT, THE PLANKTON POPULATION WILL INCREASE OUT OF CONTROL, AND THERE'LL BE A CATASTROPHIC GLOBAL TEMPERATURE RISE.
"OUR STUPIDITY HAS TURNED THE WORLD INTO A HAND GRENADE. OUR GREED HAS PULLED THE PIN."

REMEMBER DOLPHIN?

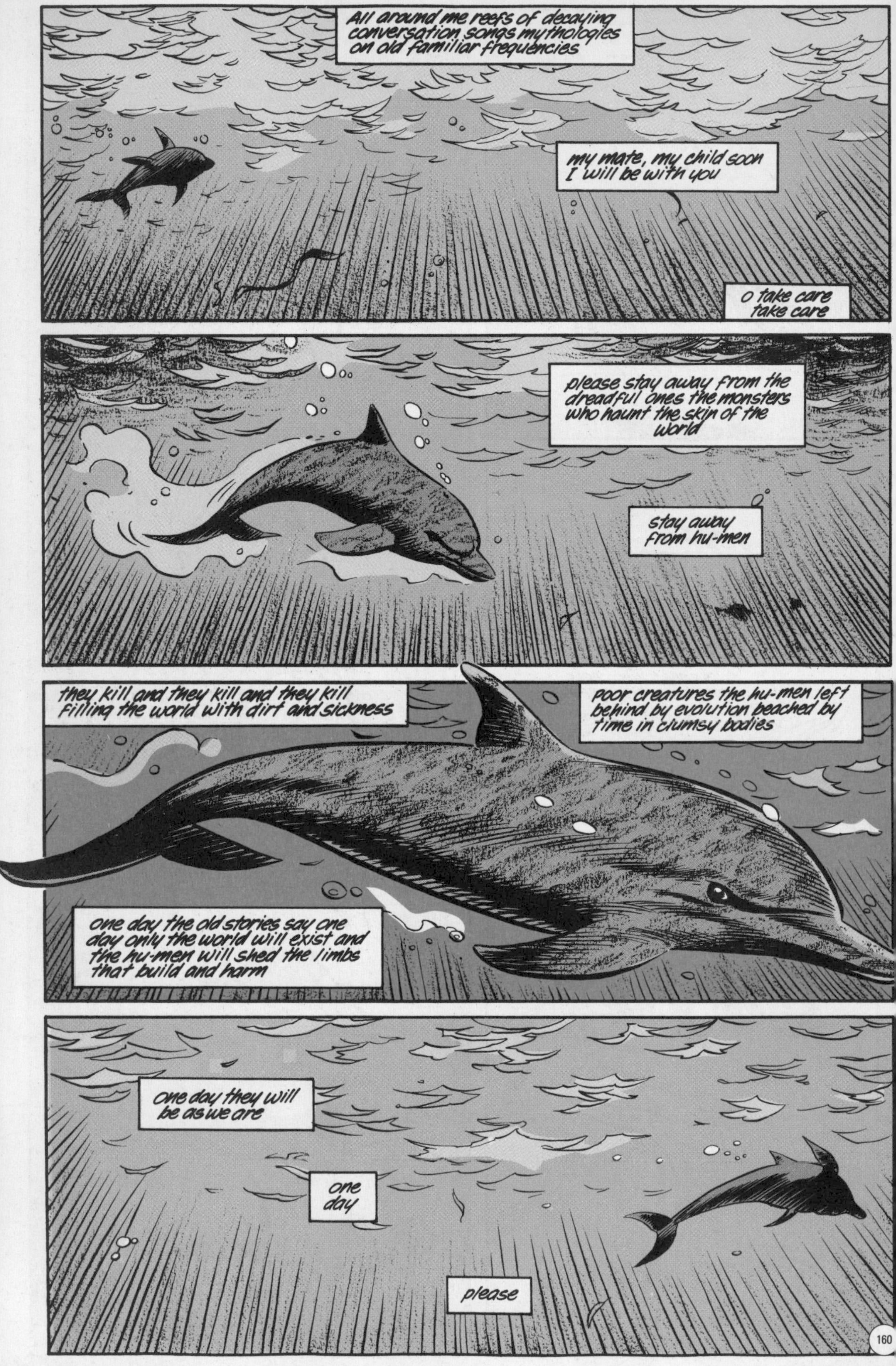
All around me reefs of decaying conversation songs mythologies on old familiar frequencies
my mate, my child soon I will be with you
o take care take care
please stay away from the dreadful ones the monsters who haunt the skin of the world
stay away from hu-men
they kill and they kill and they kill filling the world with dirt and sickness
poor creatures the hu-men left behind by evolution beached by time in clumsy bodies
one day the old stories say one day only the world will exist and the hu-men will shed the limbs that build and harm
one day they will be as we are
one day
please

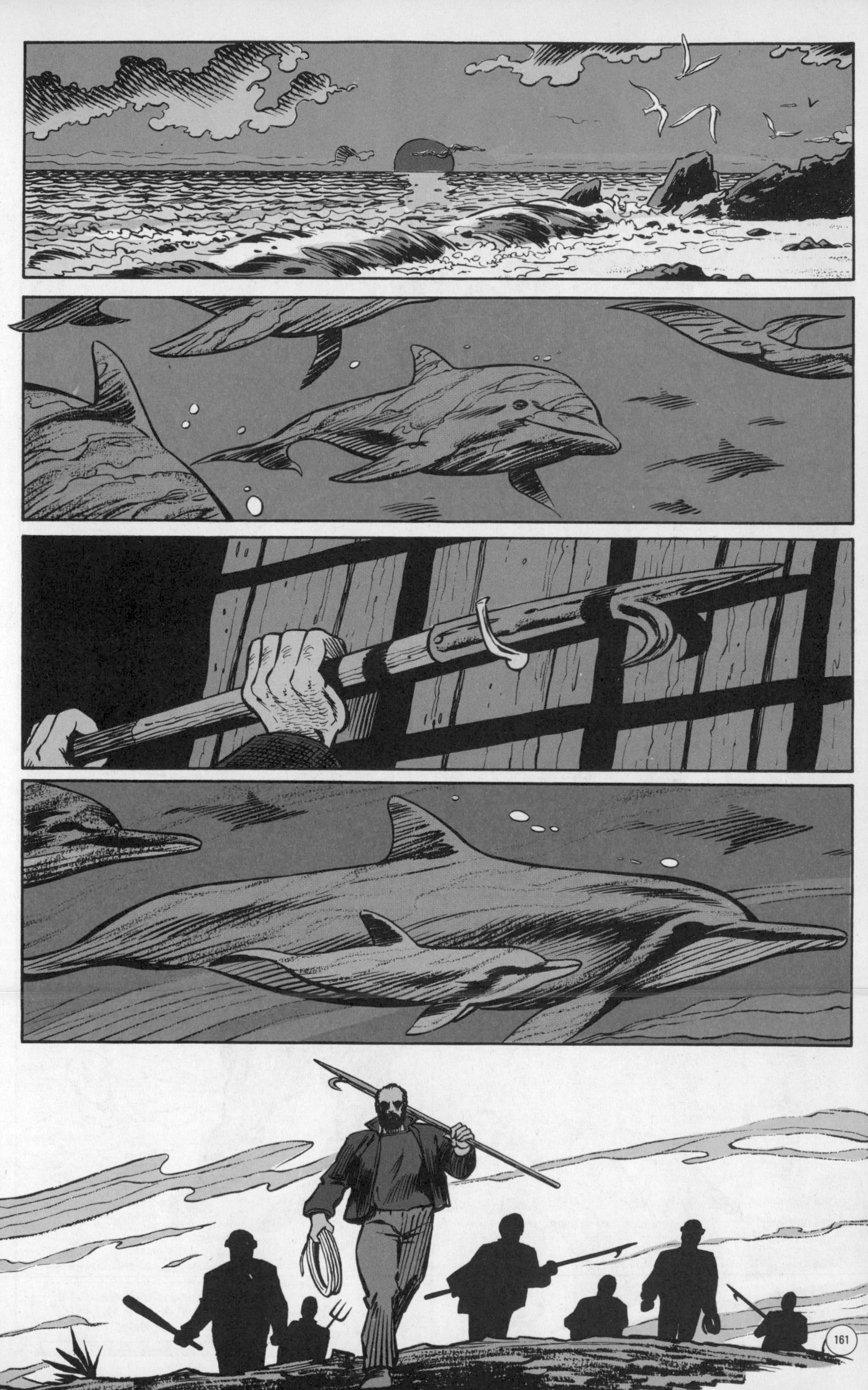

BUDDY! BUDDY, WAKE UP!
IT'S STARTED!
...WUHH...

NOW, YOU REMEMBER THE PLAN?
YEAH. SURE.

I REMEMBER THE PLAN.
"YOU AND DOLPHIN ARE OUR ACE IN THE HOLE, BUDDY.

"PROTECTING THE SCHOOL IS YOUR DEPARTMENT.
"LEAVE IT TO JOANNES AND ME TO DEAL WITH THE BAD GUYS."

THEY'RE TRYING TO DRIVE THE DOLPHINS AWAY.
WHAT DO THEY THINK I AM? AN IDIOT?

"WHAT WE NEED TO DO IS TO GET THE DOLPHINS TO DETOUR AWAY FROM THEIR USUAL ROUTES, GET THEM AWAY FROM THE COAST.

"THE MOST EFFECTIVE WAY TO DO THAT IS TO USE ULTRASOUND. TRANSMIT A WARNING SIGNAL.
"GET THEM OUT OF THE AREA AS QUICKLY AS POSSIBLE."

THE DOLPHINS ARE MOVING AWAY!
THERE'S A WAY TO KEEP THEM WHERE WE WANT THEM.
NO DOLPHIN WILL LEAVE AN INJURED COMRADE BEHIND.

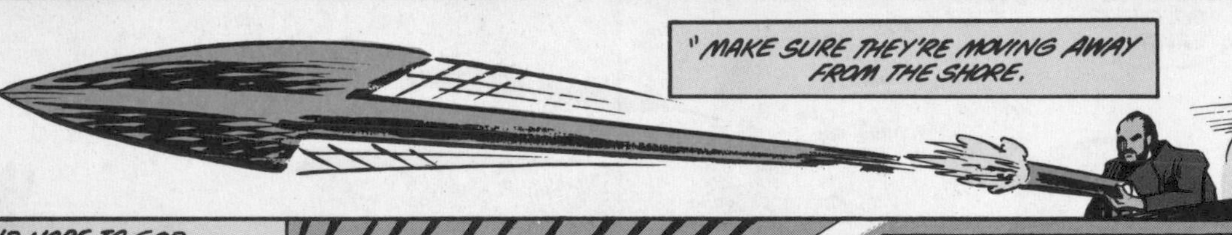

"AND HOPE TO GOD NOTHING GOES WRONG."

NOW WE DEAL WITH THE AMERICANS, EH ?
VIRGIL

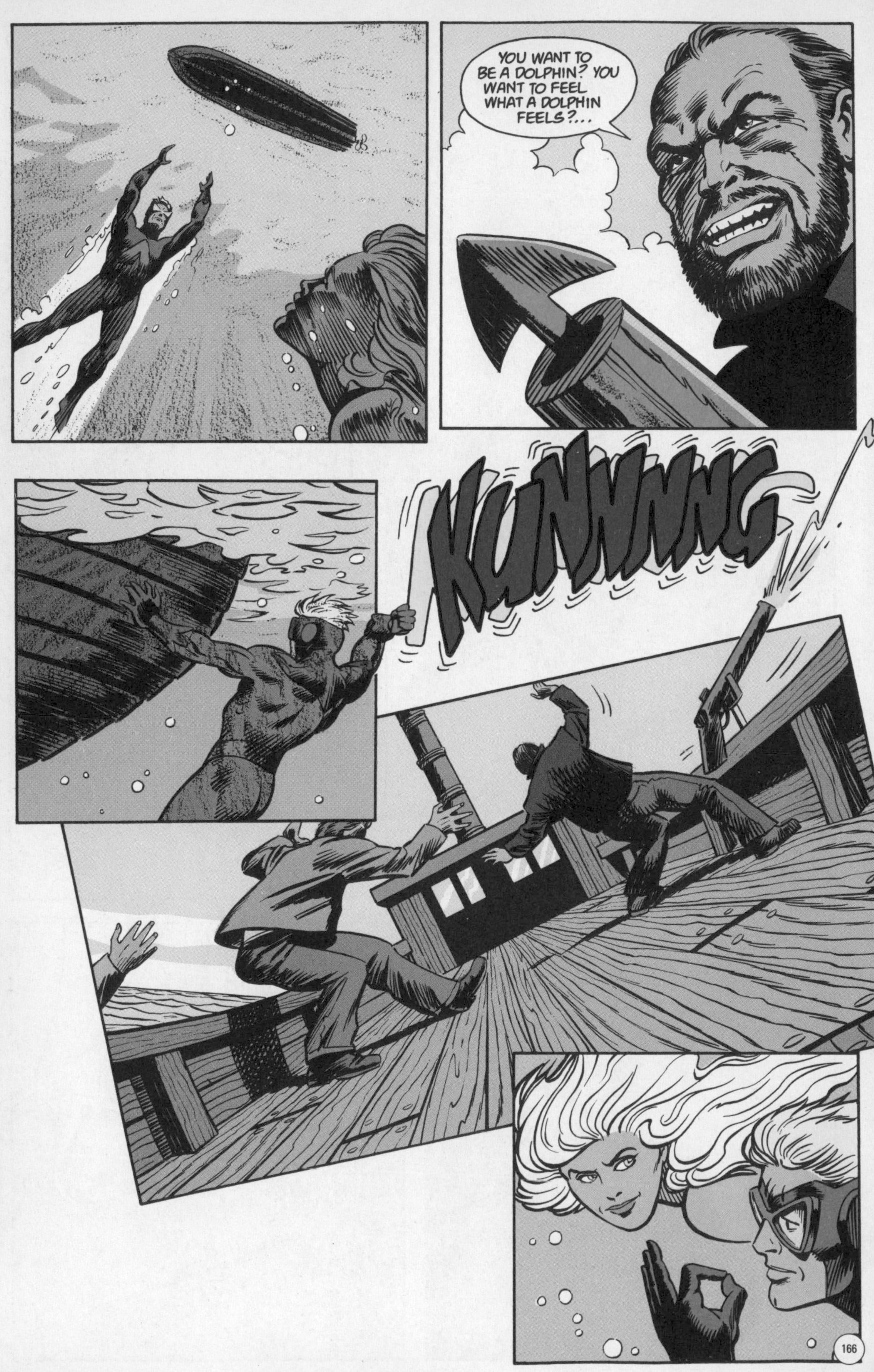
YOU WANT TO BE A DOLPHIN? YOU WANT TO FEEL WHAT A DOLPHIN FEELS?...
KUNNNNG

Panic harmonics a storm of noise and grief confusion frenzy raw dist

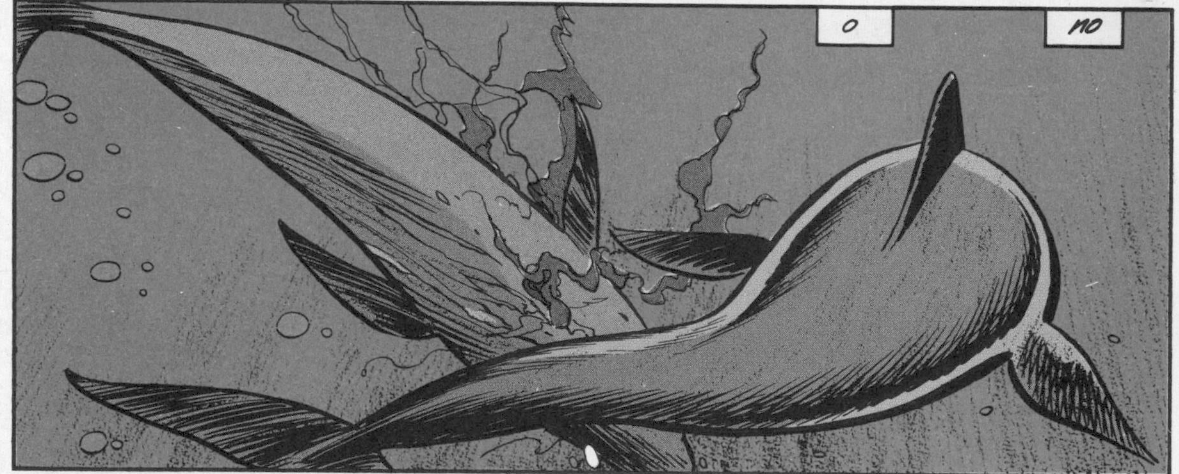
o
no

no
no

THEY'RE COMING IN!

THE DOLPHINS ARE COMING IN!

TAKE THE ONES ON THE
YAAGH!
CHUKKACHUKKACHUKK

STAY WHERE YOU ARE!
STAY RIGHT WHERE YOU ARE.

NO ONE MOVES.
I'M SERIOUS.

WHAT RIGHT DO YOU THINK YOU...
I HAVE A MORAL RIGHT.
I ALSO HAVE A LOADED MACHINE GUN...
AMERICAN!

YOU THINK YOU'RE SO CLEVER! YOU AND YOUR AMERICAN MONEY AND YOUR SUPERHEROES!
YOU THINK YOU OWN US AND CAN TELL US HOW TO LIVE, EH?

YOU LOOK! YOU SEE THIS?
THIS! THIS IS WHAT I THINK OF YOUR ENVIRONMENTALISM!

NO!

THIS!

AND THIS!
AND THIS!
AND

HUKK

OKAY.
YOU'RE FAR FROM HOME, YOU'RE OVER THE OPEN SEA...
NOW GIVE ME *ONE* REASON!
GIVE ME ONE GOOD REASON NOT TO *DROP* YOU, YOU BASTARD!
...HEIGHTS... PLEASE, I'M AFRAID OF...
I SAID ONE *GOOD* REASON.

AH, HELL! WHO CARES?

I'D DO IT ALL OVER AGAIN NEXT YEAR IF I CAN STAY OUT OF *JAIL*.

TOO BAD WE CAN'T ALL DIS-APPEAR AS EASILY AS *SHE* CAN, *EH*?

YEAH.

TOO BAD.

down
down
down
I watch him
thrashing
desperately attempting to climb to the skin of the world
blood stains his body his clumsy awkward body
thrashing
stains his frail body cradle of delicate bone stains his electrics spit and flash terror
the world is crushing him putting out the light of his body
he took everything stained with my family everything
thrashing
he will never make it back alone
he will die here
here in the world stained with our blood
he will die

one day only the world will exist no more agony no more fear in all the vast enfolding of time and the world
one day
until then the killing will continue the bloodspilling slaughter of innocents

until then there will be aggression and pain and sadness
that is the way
that is the way of the sad hu-men

our way is different

DC
NEW FORMAT
16
OCT 89
US $1.50
CAN $1.85
UK 80p
Animal Man
TM
Morrison
Truog
Hazlewood
BOLLAND

Chez Ma
Concierge
STAURANT
PSSSST!

PSSSST!
HERE.

CAN YOU TELL ME?
THE TIME.
CAN YOU TELL ME THE *TIME*?

OH,... YES, YES. IT'S... AH...
YES? IT'S *WHAT*?...
OH.

THAT'S ODD.
MY WATCH HAS *STOPPED*.
HA HA
HA

AHAHAHAHAHA

ELLEN?

ELLEN, ARE YOU *OKAY?*

ELLEN, WHAT IS IT?
BAD NEWS?

WHAT? NO, IT'S...IT'S MY *BOOK*, BUDDY.

THEY WANT TO *PUBLISH* MY BOOK.
Pacifica Publications

I CAN'T *BELIEVE* THIS.
AFTER ALL THIS TIME.
WAIT THERE.
DON'T MOVE!

HA.

OKAY. IT'S ALL FIXED!
TRICIA'S GOING TO TAKE CARE OF THE KIDS WHILE WE *CELEBRATE*!

PACK A SUITCASE.
A SUITCASE? BUDDY, WHAT'S HAPPENING?
WHERE ARE WE GOING?

PARIS.
FIVE MINUTES.

WEIRD.
THIS IS SO WEIRD.
YOU TALKING ABOUT OUR MARRIAGE AGAIN, SUE?

PROBABLY.
WHAT ARE YOU DOING HERE? I THOUGHT YOU WERE IN THE MEN'S ROOM.
I AM IN THE MEN'S ROOM.
RALPH, THAT IS GROSS.

BUT YOU LOVE ME REALLY.
SO WHAT'S SO WEIRD? APART FROM ME?
SEE FOR YOURSELF. ACCORDING TO THIS, EVERY CLOCK IN PARIS HAS STOPPED AT 11:55.

WHAT?
I TOLD YOU IT WAS WEIRD.
IS THERE ANYONE ON TRANSPORTER DUTY? SOME-ONE'S JUST BEAMED IN.

YEAH, METAMORPHO'S DOWN THERE. WHO CARES?
THIS CLOCK THING'S TERRIFIC, SUE! MY MYSTERY-LOVING NOSE IS TWITCHING ALREADY AND YOU KNOW WHAT THAT MEANS.
YEAH.
DIVORCE PROCEEDINGS.

...SO THIS IS THE JLE EMBASSY WHERE...
YOU OKAY?
YEAH... JUST A LITTLE STRANGE AFTER THAT TRANS-PORTER RIDE, LIKE I'M STONED OR SOMETHING...
MAYBE IF I SIT DOWN FOR A COUPLE OF...
YAAAA!
WAAAA
OHH... HEY, SORRY ABOUT THAT... SORRY...
SO I FELL ASLEEP IN THE SHAPE OF A CHAIR.
SO SUE ME.
YEAH... THIS IS... AH... METAMORPHO, THE ELEMENT MAN.
METAMORPHO. ELLEN.
HI THERE! YOU MUST BE THIS GUY'S WIFE!
AND RALPH DIBNY...
THE ELONGATED MAN, YOUR FLEXIBLE FRIEND!
CAUGHT NAPPING AGAIN, HUH?
YEAH... WELL, WE CAN'T ALL BE HYPERACTIVE AIRHEADS!
HYPERACTIVE? MOI?
BUDDY, THIS IS A MADHOUSE.

IT'S ALL COMING BACK.
THEY BROKE ME, BUT IT'S ALL COMING BACK.
FLYWHEELS AND COGS AND MAINSPRINGS.
ALL OF IT.
LIKE A JIGSAW.
ULTIMA FORSAN
ALL
COMING
BACK.
ULTIMA FORSAN
OH YES.

GARE

NOW I REMEMBER.
TICK TOCK TICK TOCK

AHH.

EVERYTHING FITS. SNUG AS CLOCKWORK.

YES.
THE MESH AND WHIR OF IT.
Quis custodiet ipsos custodes?

IT'S ALL COMING BACK.
EVERYTHING FITS. STILL FITS.

YES!
YES!
YES!
OH YOU HANDSOME DEVIL, YOU!

THE CLOCKWORK CRIMES of the TIME COMMANDER
LONG TIME, NO SEE.
GRANT MORRISON • writer
CHAS TRUOG and
DOUG HAZLEWOOD • artists
JOHN COSTANZA • letterer
TATJANA WOOD • colorist
ART YOUNG • assoc. editor
KAREN BERGER • editor

ISN'T THIS BEAUTIFUL, BUDDY?
YOU KNOW, WITH ALL THE RUNNING AROUND YOU'VE BEEN DOING, THIS IS THE FIRST REAL TIME WE'VE HAD TOGETHER FOR A LONG TIME.

YEAH. LISTEN, THERE'S SOMETHING I'VE BEEN MEANING TO ASK YOU, ELLEN. SOMETHING THAT'S BEEN BOTHERING ME.
DID ANYTHING STRANGE HAPPEN TO YOU WHILE I WAS IN AFRICA?
STRANGE? I DON'T THINK SO.

WELL... NO, THAT'S NOT TRUE.
I DID HAVE A KIND OF BLACK-OUT FOR A COUPLE OF MINUTES. I REMEMBER BECAUSE I SPILLED THE COFFEE...
HOW LONG WAS THAT AFTER I DISAPPEARED?
WHAT HAPPENED TO ME BEFORE THE ALIENS TOOK ME TO AFRICA?

I DON'T KNOW.
I DON'T REMEMBER YOU DISAPPEARING.
ELLEN, DON'T YOU EVER THINK THERE'S SOMETHING WEIRD ABOUT OUR LIVES?

WEIRD?
BUDDY, EVERY DAY IS WEIRD WITH YOU!

LOOK, IF I'D WANTED AN ORDINARY LIFE, I'D HAVE MARRIED A *DENTIST.* I DIDN'T. OKAY?

I DON'T KNOW HOW YOU PUT UP WITH ME SOMETIMES.

I PUT UP WITH YOU BECAUSE YOU'RE A GOOD GUY, BECAUSE YOU MAKE ME LAUGH, BECAUSE YOU HAD THE GUTS TO GO VEGETARIAN AND SEE THROUGH ALL THIS ANIMAL STUFF... I MEAN, COME *ON,* BUDDY!

HEY! KEEP GOING! I'M MAKING A *LIST!*

MAKE IT *SHORT,* PAL!

AOWW!

SO WHERE ARE WE GOING?

WELL, I FIGURED WE'D JUST DO THE USUAL TOURIST STUFF AND THEN...

WHAT'S THAT *NOISE?*

SOUNDS LIKE A...

RUE DE
HARRYHAUSEN
YIP
YIPYIP
YIP
OH WOW!

IT'S A DINOSAUR.
BUDDY!...
A REAL DINOSAUR!
STAY THERE, ELLEN!
DON'T MOVE!
ANIMAL POWERS KICK INTO GEAR... A BRIEF CHARCOAL SKETCH OF MASSIVE FORMS SCRAWLED ACROSS THE BACKBRAIN...
AND THE STOLEN STRENGTH ARRIVES LIKE A FLASHFLOOD... BIG AS A TANKER, BIG AS A BOMBER...
THUNDER IN THE HEAD.
WHOKK!
THE MONSTER'S OUT COLD BUT ITS BRAIN HASN'T YET PROCESSED THE INFORMATION... IT KEEPS WALKING.
SOUND OF EXPLODING GLASS AND SCREAMING PEOPLE... CHEMICAL SMELL OF TYRANNOSAUR DUNG...
YIP
YIP
YIP

NNNGH!

BUDDY!
BUDDY, ARE YOU OKAY?

YEAH, I'M FINE... IT'S JUST... WHAT WAS I SAYING ABOUT *WEIRDNESS* EARLIER?...
BUDDY...

LOOKS LIKE THE CAVALRY JUST GOT HERE.

TIME'S GOING CRAZY! WE'VE JUST SEEN GERMAN TANKS AND CAVEMEN CHASING JEAN PAUL SARTRE!
THE FRENCH REVOLUTION'S HAPPENING RIGHT AROUND THE CORNER!
DO WE KNOW WHAT'S CAUSING IT? I MEAN...
THE ONLY LEAD WE'VE GOT IS THE TIME WHEN ALL THE CLOCKS STOPPED--11:55. THAT'S THE TRADEMARK OF SOME GUY CALLED JOHN STARR, THE TIME COMMANDER. HE HAD A RUN-IN WITH GREEN LANTERN A FEW YEARS AGO.
HE'S PRETTY OBSCURE BUT THIS COULD BE...
BUDDY, LOOK!
LOOK AT THE DINOSAUR.
YEAH, AND CHECK THE WRECKAGE, TOO!
IT'S LIKE A FILM, RUNNING BACKWARDS.
MY GOD.
WHAT'S HAPPENING HERE?

WELL, AT LEAST *WE* DON'T HAVE TO CLEAR UP THE MESS THIS TIME.

GRAB YOUR *COSTUME* AND MEET US IN FIVE MINUTES AT THE *PLACE DE LA CONCORDE*, BUDDY.
THIS GUY'S GOT TO BE AROUND *SOMEWHERE*.
SURE.

FIVE MINUTES!
NICE TO HAVE MET YOU, MRS. BAKER.
AH... YEAH... YOU'RE *DMITRI*, RIGHT?...

YOU BET!
I JUST LOVE YOUR ENGLISH BEAT MUSIC! GERRY AND THE PACEMAKERS! THE APPLE-JACKS!
FAB GEAR!

SHUFF
IS HE *KIDDING?*
I HOPE SO.

TEMPUS·FUGIT
EXCUSE ME?
I COULDN'T HELP NOTICING... ARE YOU ALL...
OH.
YOU SEE THAT?
IT'S ME.
THAT'S ME, TEN MINUTES INTO THE FUTURE. MY NOSE IS BROKEN.
THAT'S WHAT'S GOING TO HAPPEN TO ME. SOON.
WHY DOES EVERYTHING ALWAYS TURN OUT TO BE SUCH A MESS?
I LIKE TO THINK THAT I CONTROL TIME, BUT REALLY, TIME IS LIKE A WILD HORSE. ALL YOU CAN DO IS GET ON AND RIDE UNTIL YOU FALL OFF.
I'M FALLING OFF NOW. I'M FALLING AND I'M GOING TO HIT BOTTOM AND ALL THE CLOCKWORK IN MY HEAD WILL BREAK.
I CAN'T FACE PRISON AGAIN.
PSYCHIATRISTS WITH HAMMERS. CLUMSY. BREAKING ME INTO BITS.
THEY MADE ME FORGET BUT THEN I REMEMBERED AND ALL THE CLOCKS STOPPED. IT WAS A SIGN.
MY HOURGLASS WAS CALLING. MY MAGICAL, BEAUTIFUL HOURGLASS. "TODAY," IT SAID. "TODAY WE WILL CHANGE THE WORLD."
WE'RE CHANGING IT ALREADY.
WHO ARE THOSE FLOWERS FOR?

MY HUSBAND... THEY'RE FOR MY HUSBAND.
I ALWAYS TRY TO BRING SOMETHING. HE DIED NOT LONG AFTER WE WERE MARRIED. CANCER. IN THE BRAIN...
BUT THERE IS NO DEATH!
LOVE DENIES ENTROPY! THROUGH LOVE, WE ABOLISH DEATH!
FEEL IT.
YEARS FALL AWAY.
FALL BECOMES SUMMER, SUMMER WINDS BACK INTO SPRING. ALL THE BIRDS ARE SINGING! ALL THE LOVE IN THE WORLD!
FEEL IT!
OH.
LOOK.
JEAN-LOUIS?
MY FATHER... MY DEAR DAD... ALL I WANT IS AN HOUR... HALF AN HOUR...
THEY'RE ALL COMING BACK. ALL THE LOST, LOVED ONES.
NO MORE SADNESS! NO MORE BEREAVEMENT! NO MORE SUPERHEROES AND DOCTORS WITH HAMMERS!
EVERYTHING FITS, EVERYTHING IS BEAUTIFUL!
AND LOVE LOVE LOVE IS THE CLOCKWORK THAT TURNS THE WORLD!
STARR.

IT'S OVER.
IT'S ALL OVER.

PRISON BARS?
YOU CAN'T HOLD *ME* IN PRISON BARS. I'M THE *TIME COMMANDER*!
CHUNT

I CAN SLIP *SIDEWAYS* THROUGH THE HOURS...

...THROUGH THE MINUTES, THROUGH THE SECONDS!
TIME, WHICH SETS *YOU* LIKE CEMENT, IS *CLAY* IN MY HANDS.

FOR INSTANCE!...
YAAA

AAAAAA

WUFF!
FROM SOME FAR-AWAY STREET COMES THE LONG CRY OF A SABRE-TOOTH... A GUILLOTINE BLADE RINGS DOWN...

BIPLANES BUZZ ACROSS BLUE, BLUE SKIES... THE DEAD AND THE LIVING ARE REUNITED...
AND TIME IS SET FREE.

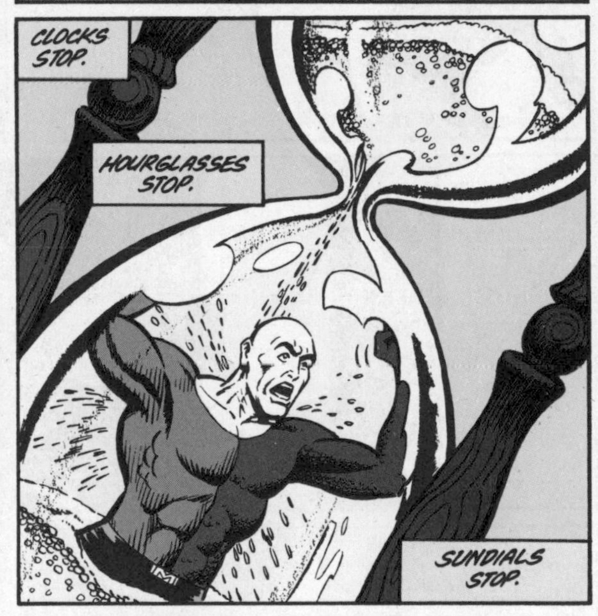
CLOCKS STOP.
HOURGLASSES STOP.
SUNDIALS STOP.

THE YEARS AND THE SEASONS ARE SHUFFLED LIKE PLAYING CARDS.
BLOSSOM SHOWERS OUT OF THE TREES... PERFUMED CONFETTI FOR THE ALCHEMICAL WEDDING OF TIME TO TIME... THERE IS NO MORE DEATH, NOR ANY SORROW...
THE PAST IS NO LONGER ANOTHER COUNTRY.

SO. DO YOU WANT TO FIGHT ME, TOO?
DO YOU WANT TO TRY TO HIT ME?

NO. NOT REALLY. JUST BECAUSE I WEAR A COSTUME DOESN'T MEAN I ENJOY FIGHTING.
I'M JUST A LITTLE CONCERNED ABOUT WHAT YOU'RE DOING HERE. MAYBE YOU SHOULD THINK ABOUT IT.
THINK? THINK? THINKING JUST CLOGS THE CLOCK-WORK... I...
PEOPLE LIKE ME MAKE THE WORLD MORE INTERESTING... GIANT SUNDIALS, DINOSAURS AND HOURGLASSES MADE OF LIGHT...
I'M NOT DOING ANYTHING WRONG, AM I?
WELL, YOU CAN'T JUST TAKE IT INTO YOUR OWN HANDS TO...
I DON'T REALLY THINK YOU'RE A BAD PERSON, WHOEVER YOU ARE, BUT YOU'RE STILL ON THEIR SIDE. ON THE SIDE OF THE HAMMERS. ON THE SIDE OF THE DOCTORS WHO BREAK ALL THE BEAUTIFUL THINGS AND DRINK OUR TEARS.
THEY DON'T UNDER-STAND LOVE.
THEY'LL UNDER-STAND NOW.
THE FINAL TRANSFOR...
SKLEEESH!
YOU WERE SAYING?

NO... I COULD HAVE TURNED IT ALL BACK... I COULD HAVE TAKEN US ALL BACK TO THE GARDEN.
TO THE GARDEN OF EDEN...

ULTIMA FORSAN

METAMORPHO... METAMORPHO, WAIT!
DON'T HIT HIM...

ULTIMA FORSAN

TICK TOCK TICK... NO NO NO!
STOP THE SIREN! THE HAMMERS SMASHING!
STOP IT!

FORSAN

STOP! OH GOD, STOP THEM BREAKING.
BREAKING IT ALL.
CRASH CRASH CRASH!

...DON'T...

WHUTTCH

JEAN-LOUIIIS!

BUDDY, I'M IMPRESSED!

YOUR FRENCH IS IMPROVING.
WHAT'S THE MATTER? WHAT ARE YOU THINKING?
ABOUT THAT GUY TODAY. THE TIME COMMANDER.
I DON'T KNOW.

YOU CAN'T ALWAYS DO THE RIGHT THING...
YEAH.
LET'S NOT TALK ABOUT IT. THIS IS YOUR NIGHT, ELLEN.

I MEAN, YOU'VE SOLD YOUR BOOK, IT'S GOING TO BE A MILLION SELLER, YOUR HUSBAND'S IN THE JUSTICE LEAGUE, THE KIDS ARE DOING FINE...
I KNOW. IT'S ALL WORKING OUT, ISN'T IT?
EVERYTHING'S WORKING OUT.

EVERYTHING'S GOING TO BE ALL RIGHT.

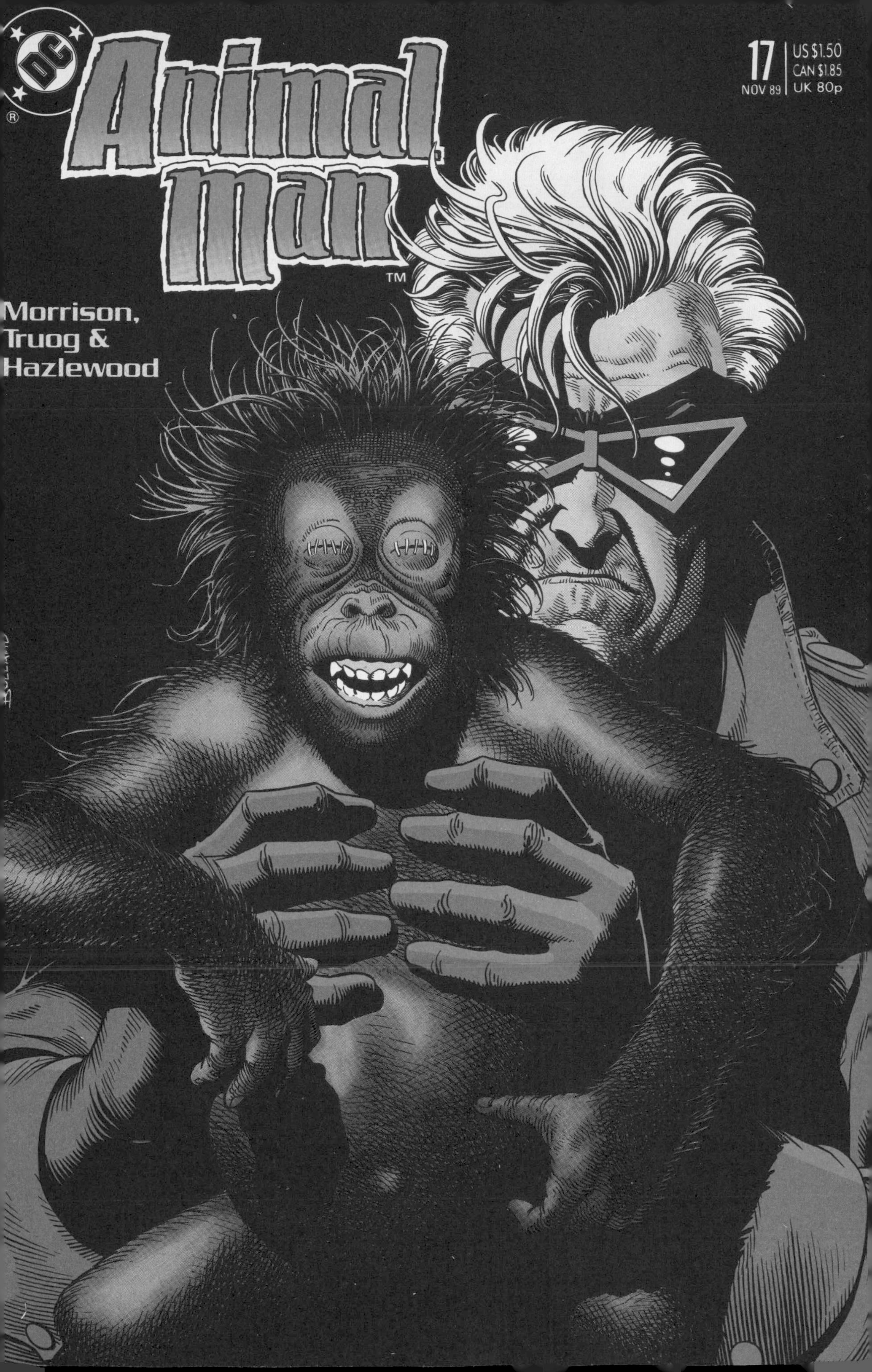
DC
Animal Man
17
NOV 89
US $1.50
CAN $1.85
UK 80p
Morrison,
Truog &
Hazlewood
BOLLAND

WELL?...

I'M HERE.

WHAT'S THE MATTER, McCULLOCH?
ARE YOU GOING TO ANSWER ME OR NOT?

ANSWER ME, McCULLOCH!
I DIDN'T TRAVEL THOUSANDS OF MILES TO PLAY TRICKS!
McCULLOCH, DID YOU...
HAHAHA

NEVER MIND THE "McCULLOCH"...

IT'S THE MIRROR MASTER TO YOU, JIM.
AWRIGHT?

SO HOWZITGAUN?
SHOT ANYBODY INTERESTING?

DON'T WASTE MY TIME.
YOU KNOW WHY I'M HERE.

HOW D'YOU FANCY THIS PLACE, EH?
THE NECROPOLIS, WE CALL IT. THE DEAD CENTER OF GLASGOW, GET IT?

AYE. I THOUGHT THAT MIGHT RAISE A SMILE.

SO WHAT'S THE STORY ABOUT YOU TAKING OVER THE ANIMAL MAN JOB?
I'M BOMBED OUT, AM I?

YOUR SERVICES ARE NO LONGER REQUIRED, IF THAT'S WHAT YOU'RE TRYING TO SAY.
OH, IS THAT RIGHT, IS IT?
SINCE WHEN?

SINCE YOU TURNED OUT TO BE SO SQUEAMISH.
OH AYE, IT TAKES A REAL HARD TICKET LIKE YOU TO DEAL WITH A COUPLE OF KIDS AND A WOMAN...

THIS IS A JOB FOR A PROFESSIONAL, NOT FOR SOME SMALL-TIME THUG FROM THE ASSHOLE OF THE WORLD.
YOU TALKING ABOUT GLASGOW?
YOU TALKING ABOUT THE EUROPEAN CITY OF CULTURE 1990?

'CAUSE IF YOU ARE, YOU'RE ASKING FOR A MOUTHFUL OF DANDRUFF, PAL...
YOU'RE WASTING MY TIME, McCULLOCH, AND WHERE I COME FROM, TIME IS MONEY. SERIOUS MONEY.
YOU KNOW WHAT I WANT.

THE LAYOUT, McCULLOCH.
THE LAYOUT OF ANIMAL MAN'S HOUSE.

SIDE LABORATORIES
SITY OF CALIFORNIA
NO
RESPASSING

PERMIT PARKING ONLY

THRUNNCH

HERE.
IN HERE.

CONSEQUENCES
GRANT MORRISON writer • CHAS TRUOG and DOUG HAZLEWOOD artists
JOHN COSTANZA letterer • TATJANA WOOD colorist • ART YOUNG assoc. editor
KAREN BERGER, editor
MY GOD.
GASO

OH MY GOD.

WHY HAVE THEY *DONE* THIS?

SIGHT DEPRIVATION EXPERIMENTS.

TOTALLY WORTHLESS.

KHRRENK

THESE MONKEYS SPEND THEIR ENTIRE LIVES IN DARKNESS AND THEN THEY'RE *KILLED*.

WHAT ABOUT THEIR EYES?
CAN WE SAVE THEM?

I HOPE SO, YEAH. WE HAVE VETERINARIANS WHO'LL BE WILLING TO HELP US.
WE ALSO HAVE SUPPORTERS WHO OWN FARMS AND RANCHES. THE ANIMALS ARE TAKEN CARE OF THERE.

NOW, COME ON! LET'S MOVE OUT!
LOG

WHAT ARE YOU GOING TO DO?
I DON'T THINK YOU SHOULD...
ANIMAL MAN, JUST GET THE MONKEYS OUT, HUH?
I KNOW WHAT I'M DOING.

AND I WANT THEM TO KNOW WHY I'M DOING IT!

FWUMMF

A 747 CRASH IN MEXICO... THREE FIREMEN INJURED IN A CHEMICAL BLAZE... DROWNED CHILDREN...
THE RADIO HAS ONLY BAD NEWS TO TELL ME. I PAN ACROSS THE WAVEBANDS, LISTEN TO WHITE NOISE.

WHY IS THERE SO MUCH SUFFERING IN THE WORLD?
I KNOW WHY. I KNOW NOW WHAT THE PSYCHO-PIRATE KNOWS.
I KNOW WHY THERE IS SUFFERING.

AND I KNOW WHY IT IS SUDDENLY FALL... I KNOW WHY MY NAME IS JAMES HIGHWATER AND WHERE THIS CAR CAME FROM AND WHY I HAVE TO FIND ANIMAL MAN AND
AND

YAAAAAA!

I KNOW!

IN JUST 7 DAYS, I CAN PUMP YOU UP!
THE TREMENDOUS TACHYON MAN
1ST ISSUE!
CLIFF.
WAUUU
FASTER THAN A TACHYON!
POW
BLAM!
HI, CLIFF.
WHAT WAS THAT YOU WERE *EATING*?
WHAT?...
...*UM*... IT WAS *NOTHING*, DAD...
NOTHING.
IT'S... *AH*...
IT'S A BURGER.
I KNOW. I COULD *SMELL* IT.
CLIFF, WE'RE SUPPOSED TO BE *VEGETARIANS*...
I'M *SICK* OF BEING A VEGETARIAN!
EVERYBODY THINKS I'M *WEIRD*...

HOW COME EVERYONE ELSE EATS MEAT? ALL THE GUYS AT SCHOOL EAT MEAT.
EVEN THE CAT EATS MEAT!
CATS HAVE TO EAT MEAT OR THEY DIE.
HUMANS ARE DIFFERENT.
HUMANS CAN THINK THINGS THROUGH. YOU'VE GOT TO UNDERSTAND THAT NOTHING EXISTS IN A VACUUM, CLIFF. EVERYTHING IS CONNECTED.
CERTAIN EVENTS HAVE CERTAIN CONSEQUENCES.
I MEAN, WHEN YOU EAT A BURGER, RIGHT?... YOU'RE CONTRIBUTING TO THE DESTRUCTION OF THE RAINFORESTS.
MASSIVE AREAS OF FOREST GET CLEARED EVERY DAY TO PROVIDE GRAZING LAND FOR THE CATTLE THAT GET TURNED INTO BURGERS.
THOSE FORESTS ARE THE LUNGS OF THE WORLD. WHEN THEY'RE GONE, THE CARBON DIOXIDE LEVELS WILL GO WAY UP.
THAT'S THE GREENHOUSE EFFECT AND IT'S ALREADY HAPPENING.
EVERY TIME YOU EAT A BURGER, YOU'RE HELPING TO KILL THE WORLD.
EVERYTHING'S CONNECTED, THAT'S ALL I'M TRYING TO SAY. THAT'S WHY I DO WHAT I DO.
I DON'T WANT TO SEE YOU AND MAXINE GROWING UP ON A DYING PLANET.
I CAN'T FORCE YOU NOT TO EAT MEAT, CLIFF. I DON'T WANT TO FORCE YOU.
I JUST WANT YOU TO THINK ABOUT THINGS, THAT'S ALL.

WELL?...
WELL, WHAT?

THE LAYOUT OF THE HOUSE. I NEED THE LAYOUT OF THE HOUSE.
YOU THINK MY HEAD'S BUTTONED UP THE BACK? YOU THINK I CAME UP THE CLYDE ON A BIKE?
AWAY AND CHASE YOURSELF!

I THOUGHT YOU MIGHT SAY THAT.

CHHSH

AAAA

YOU'LL NOT DO THAT AGAIN IN A HURRY, EH?

HI, ELLEN!

WHERE DID YOU FIND THE BLACK ONE?
I HAVEN'T SEEN THAT SINCE I WAS 21...
BUDDY, HAVE YOU SEEN THE NEWS?

WHY? WHAT'S ON THE NEWS?...
THREE FIREMEN WERE HURT LAST NIGHT. IN THE ANIMAL LABORATORIES AT CALIFORNIA UNIVERSITY.
IT WAS A CHEMICAL FIRE. ONE OF THE MEN IS CRITICAL.

WE'RE NOT TALKING ABOUT EVIL EXPERI-MENTS OR ANIMAL TORTURERS. THESE WERE JUST GUYS DOING THEIR JOB.

FIREMEN, BUDDY.

OH GOD.

DADDY! GORILLA MILLER SAYS HE WANTS TO TELL YOU A SECRET...
TELL HIM I'LL TALK TO HIM LATER, MAXINE.
MAYBE LATER.
I'VE GONE ALONG WITH THIS ANIMAL RIGHTS STUFF BUDDY.
I HAVEN'T SAID ANYTHING BECAUSE I AGREE WITH YOU.
UP TO A POINT.
AND YOU JUST CROSSED THE LINE.
THOSE PEOPLE YOU'RE HANGING OUT WITH ARE DANGEROUS. THEY DON'T WANT TO HELP ANIMALS, THEY JUST WANT TO HURT PEOPLE.
THOSE FIREMEN HAVE FAMILIES, TOO.
ELLEN...I...
I JUST SPOKE TO ROGER. HE SAYS HE WANTS TO TALK TO YOU.
HE SAYS YOU'LL KNOW THE PLACE.

BUDDY.
ROGER.

I HOPE YOU REMEMBERED YOU'RE SUPPOSED TO BE DOING THAT TV *DEBATE* TOMORROW...

OF COURSE I REMEMBERED.
YOU DIDN'T COME UP HERE JUST TO TELL ME *THAT*, DID YOU?
NO, I GUESS I *DIDN'T*.

IT'S FUNNY.
THIS IS WHERE IT ALL *STARTED*, BUDDY. TEN YEARS AGO.

YOU WERE LUCKY. A SPACESHIP BLEW UP IN YOUR FACE AND YOU GOT ANIMAL POWERS...
WHAT ARE YOU TRYING TO SAY, ROGER?

A WHOLE ROOM BLEW UP IN THAT FIREMAN'S FACE. HE DIDN'T GET SPECIAL POWERS.
HE GOT EIGHTY PERCENT BURNS.

HOW DID IT END UP LIKE THIS, BUDDY?
IT DIDN'T START OUT THIS WAY.

"IT WAS ALL A BIG JOKE, REMEMBER? YOU FOUND YOURSELF WITH ANIMAL POWERS, THEN I FOUND A SECOND SPACESHIP.
"IT WASN'T ANY BIG HEAVY DEAL.

RAMONES
"WE JUST WANTED A FEW LAUGHS.

"AND ELLEN'S DAD USED TO COMPLAIN BECAUSE YOU MADE HER BUY THE SEX PISTOLS ALBUM, AND WE TRIED TO START THAT BAND WITH JUST ONE GUITAR AND A COUPLE OF SONGS ABOUT ANARCHY...
"NO BIG DEAL. ANIMAL POWERS WERE JUST PART OF THE FUN.
RAMONES

"ALIEN INVASION? SURE! ANYTHING FOR A FEW LAUGHS.
"AND THEN WHEN YOU FIRST HAD THE ANIMAL MAN COSTUME MADE... YOU ONLY DID IT BECAUSE YOU THOUGHT YOU COULD RAISE SOME MONEY TO BUY A DRUM KIT...
"EVERY COUPLE OF MONTHS YOU'D STOP SOME GUYS ROBBING THE PET STORE OR SOMETHING. I MEAN, IT WAS NICE AND SIMPLE THEN, BUDDY.
"NOW I DON'T KNOW WHETHER YOU'RE A SUPER-HERO OR A SUPER-VILLAIN..."
IT'S GONE TOO FAR AND PEOPLE ARE STARTING TO GET HURT.
I'M STILL YOUR FRIEND, OKAY? BUT I DON'T WANT TO BE YOUR MANAGER ANYMORE.
YEAH. OKAY. THAT'S OKAY, BECAUSE I DON'T THINK I WANT TO BE ANIMAL MAN ANYMORE EITHER.
I'M 30 YEARS OLD, ROGER. I DON'T WANT TO SPEND MY LIFE BEATING ON GUYS IN TIGHTS WHO WANT TO RULE THE WORLD.
I DIDN'T WANT TO BE LIKE ALL THOSE OTHER "SUPERHEROES," YOU KNOW? I WANTED TO MAKE A DIFFERENCE...
THE REAL SUPER-VILLAINS DON'T WANT TO RULE THE WORLD, THEY ALREADY DO.
BUSINESSMEN IN SUITS... MULTINATIONALS... BIG CORPORATIONS...
MY GOD, LISTEN TO YOURSELF, BUDDY!
YOU DON'T HAVE CONVERSATIONS ANYMORE, YOU GIVE LECTURES!

DON'T YOU THINK I KNOW HOW I SOUND...I...IT'S JUST ALL THIS STUFF THAT'S GOING WRONG IN THIS WORLD.
I JUST GET SO...SO FRUSTRATED...

THE OZONE LAYER'S BREAKING UP. THE WHALES AND THE DOLPHINS ARE DYING.
POACHERS HAVE BROUGHT THE ELEPHANTS CLOSE TO EXTINCTION. THE CHIMPANZEES AND THE TIGERS ARE ALMOST GONE...
ALL THOSE VICIOUS... POINTLESS EXPERIMENTS...
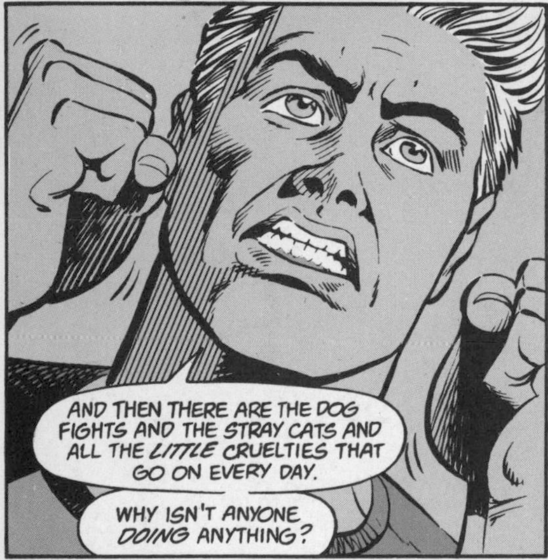
AND THEN THERE ARE THE DOG FIGHTS AND THE STRAY CATS AND ALL THE LITTLE CRUELTIES THAT GO ON EVERY DAY.
WHY ISN'T ANYONE DOING ANYTHING?

THESE THINGS DRIVE ME INSANE, ROGER. THEY REALLY DO. BUT I'M ONLY ONE MAN.
I DO WHAT I CAN.

AND THIS TIME YOU DID THE WRONG THING, BUDDY.

YEAH.
GUESS I DID.

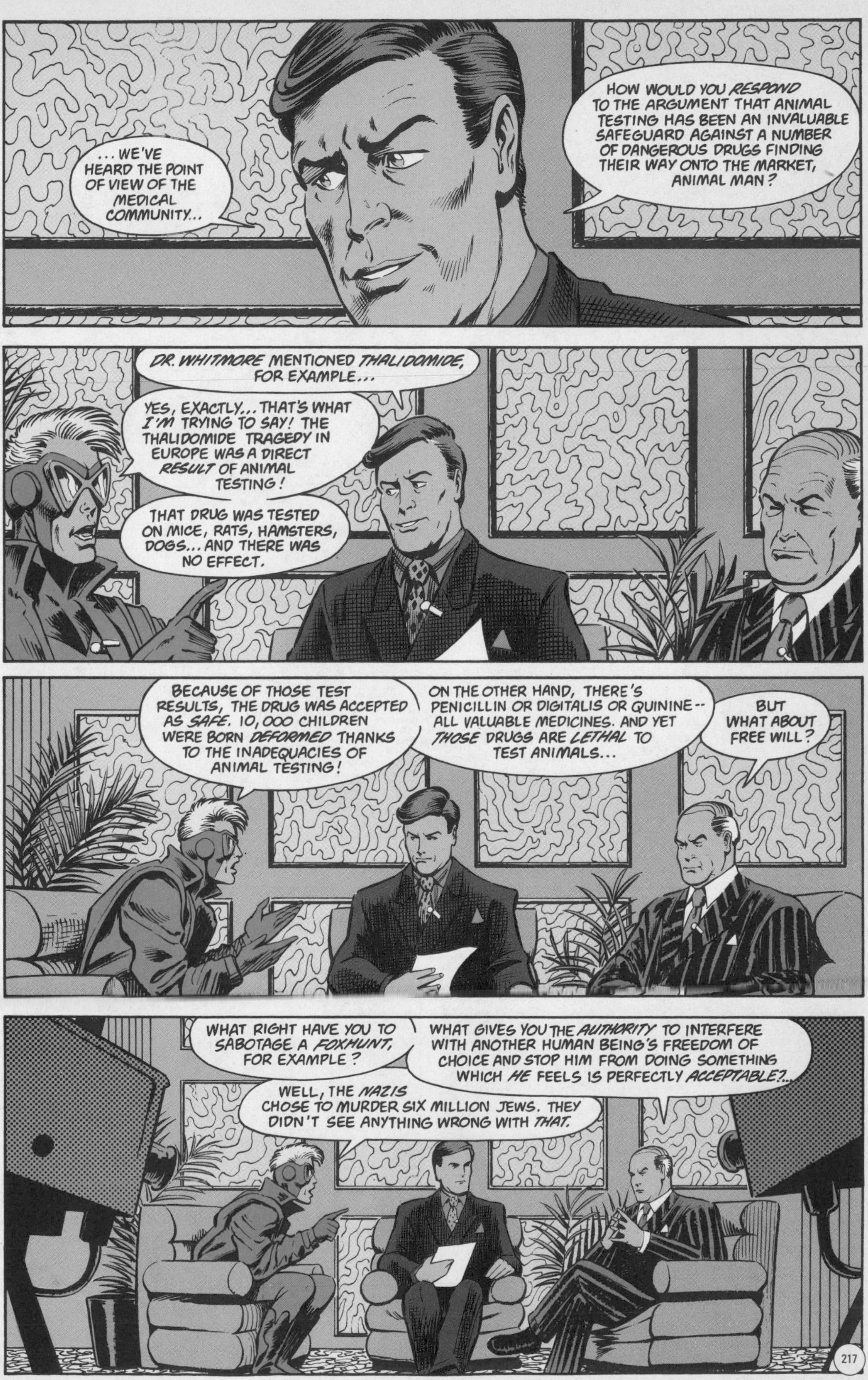

... WE'VE HEARD THE POINT OF VIEW OF THE MEDICAL COMMUNITY...
HOW WOULD YOU *RESPOND* TO THE ARGUMENT THAT ANIMAL TESTING HAS BEEN AN INVALUABLE SAFEGUARD AGAINST A NUMBER OF DANGEROUS DRUGS FINDING THEIR WAY ONTO THE MARKET, ANIMAL MAN?

DR. WHITMORE MENTIONED *THALIDOMIDE*, FOR EXAMPLE...
YES, EXACTLY... THAT'S WHAT *I'M* TRYING TO SAY! THE THALIDOMIDE TRAGEDY IN EUROPE WAS A DIRECT *RESULT* OF ANIMAL TESTING!
THAT DRUG WAS TESTED ON MICE, RATS, HAMSTERS, DOGS... AND THERE WAS NO EFFECT.

BECAUSE OF THOSE TEST RESULTS, THE DRUG WAS ACCEPTED AS *SAFE*. 10,000 CHILDREN WERE BORN *DEFORMED* THANKS TO THE INADEQUACIES OF ANIMAL TESTING!
ON THE OTHER HAND, THERE'S PENICILLIN OR DIGITALIS OR QUININE -- ALL VALUABLE MEDICINES. AND YET *THOSE* DRUGS ARE *LETHAL* TO TEST ANIMALS...
BUT WHAT ABOUT FREE WILL?

SHOULD WE HAVE ALLOWED HITLER TO CONTINUE WHAT HE WAS DOING JUST BECAUSE HE THOUGHT IT WAS ACCEPTABLE?
SO YOU'RE COMPARING JEWS TO ANIMALS, IS THAT IT?...
OF COURSE I'M NOT AND YOU KNOW IT! YOU'RE JUST TWISTING MY WORDS...
ALL I'M SAYING IS THAT MORAL LAWS ARE MORE IMPORTANT THAN THE LAW OF THE LAND.

ARE YOU SAYING THEN THAT YOU SET YOURSELF ABOVE "THE LAW OF THE LAND"? IS THAT WHAT YOU'RE SAYING?
WOULD YOU BREAK THE LAW?

...YES...
IF I THOUGHT THE LAW WAS MORALLY WRONG, I GUESS I WOULD...

AND YOU SIT THERE, WEARING THAT COSTUME, KNOWING FULL WELL THAT YOU ARE A ROLE MODEL TO COUNTLESS AMERICAN CHILDREN?
LET ME PUT THIS TO YOU...

HAVE YOU BROKEN THE LAW?

I DON'T SEE HOW THAT HAS ANYTHING AT ALL TO DO WITH YOU! YOU'RE JUST AVOIDING THE REAL ISSUES HERE!
I MEAN... WHAT I DO AS AN INDIVIDUAL HAS ABSOLUTELY NOTHING TO DO WITH WHAT WE'RE REALLY SUPPOSED TO BE DISCUSSING HERE!

I REFUSE TO BE SET UP AS A ROLE MODEL! FOR CHILDREN OR ANYONE ELSE! I DO WHAT I THINK IS RIGHT! IT HAS NOTHING TO DO WITH YOU!

I'M NOT SUPERMAN! I'M JUST A MAN AND I MAKE MISTAKES LIKE ANYONE ELSE!
AND JUST BECAUSE I WEAR A COSTUME DOESN'T MEAN I ALWAYS HAVE TO BE RIGHT!

I THINK THAT OUTBURST SAYS IT ALL, DON'T YOU?

WHERE ARE YOU, McCULLOCH?
WHAT ARE YOU DOING?
SEE MY MAGIC MIRRORS? PURE DEAD BRILLIANT, SO THEY ARE.
SEE ME? FULL OF TRICKS.
YOU COME HERE THINKING YOU'RE SOME BIG MAN? YOU THINK WE'RE ALL GOING TO DROP A CARAMEL 'CAUSE YOU'VE GOT A REPUTATION?
YOU'RE NOT IN CALIFORNIA NOW. THIS IS GLASGOW, PAL. CATCH MY DRIFT?
EH?
HOWZITGAUN, WEE MAN?
IF YOU WANT THE LAYOUT OF THAT GUY'S HOUSE YOU CAN WHISTLE FOR IT.
TELL THAT TO YOUR BOSSES AS WELL.
YOU'VE NOT HEARD THE END OF THIS, PAL.
NOT BY A LONG CHALK.

...SO WHAT ARE YOU SAYING? YOU DON'T WANT TO HELP US ANYMORE? IS THAT IT?
LOOK, I GOT INTO THIS TO HELP ABUSED ANIMALS, NOT TO INJURE INNOCENT PEOPLE...

NOBODY WANTS TO SEE ANYONE GET HURT, BUT THIS ISN'T KID STUFF, ANIMAL MAN!
THIS IS WAR.
THEN I'M NOT A SOLDIER.
I WON'T BE A SOLDIER.

AS A MATTER OF FACT, I'M NOT EVEN ANIMAL MAN ANYMORE. I'M RESIGNING FROM THE JLE AND THROWING AWAY MY COSTUMES.
AND I'M SENDING MY LAST WAGE PACKET TO THAT FIREMAN IN THE HOSPITAL. MAYBE HE CAN BUY SOME STRAWS TO EAT THROUGH...

COME ON, MAN! WE NEED YOU! I MEAN, YOU'VE BECOME, LIKE, A FIGUREHEAD FOR THE WHOLE ANIMAL RIGHTS MOVEMENT!
I'M NOT A FIGUREHEAD. I'M NOT A SPOKESMAN. I'M JUST A MAN.
ANIMAL MAN IS FINISHED. I'VE HAD ENOUGH.

WAIT A MINUTE!
FOR GOD'S SAKE, JUST...

...WAIT...

SAN

BUDDY! HURRY!
WHAT'S UP? WHAT'S THE MATTER?

ELLEN, WHAT'S WRONG?
IN THE HOUSE!
HE'S IN THE HOUSE!

NOT AGAIN!

HELP...

NEXT: At Play in the Fields of the Lord